Crypto Renaissance
Navigating the Bull Run of 2025

Table of Contents

Introduction 4

Chapter 1 Introduction to the Crypto Renaissance 7

    The Evolution of Cryptocurrency 8

    Why 2025 Marks a New Era 11

    The Impact of Blockchain Technology 13

Chapter 2 Understanding Market Cycles 18

    The Phases of a Bull Run 19

    Identifying Market Trends 22

    Lessons from Previous Bull Runs 25

Chapter 3 Preparing for the Bull Run 29

    Building a Solid Foundation: Risk Management 30

    The Role of Technical Analysis 33

    Developing a Winning Strategy 37

Chapter 4 The Role of Institutional Investors 41

    Mainstream Adoption of Crypto 42

    Institutional Investment Vehicles 46

    The Ripple Effect on Market Dynamics 50

Chapter 5 Key Cryptocurrencies to Watch 55

    Bitcoin: The Market Leader 56

    Ethereum: Innovation Beyond Smart Contracts 59

    Emerging Altcoins with High Potential 63

Chapter 6 The Bull Run Begins: Timing and Entry Points 67

Spotting Early Indicators of a Bull Market................................. 68

Analyzing Buy Signals 72

Making Your First Investment During the Run 75

Chapter 7 Navigating Volatility 79

Understanding Market Fluctuations 80

The Psychology of Crypto Trading 84

Staying Calm During Market Corrections 88

Chapter 8: Risk Management Strategies for the Bull Run. 92

Diversification: Spreading the Risk 93

Setting Stop-Loss Orders 97

Taking Profits at the Right Time 100

Chapter 9 The Role of Decentralized Finance (DeFi) 104

DeFi: What It Means for the Crypto Ecosystem...................... 105

Lending, Borrowing, and Yield Farming 109

How DeFi Can Accelerate the Bull Run................................... 112

Conclusion 116

Introduction

The cryptocurrency market has seen exponential growth since its inception, evolving from an experimental digital asset into a major financial force. Yet, despite its rapid rise, the true potential of cryptocurrency has only begun to be realized. The year 2025 marks a pivotal moment in the digital currency ecosystem — a period that many believe will signal a new era of innovation, wealth creation, and mainstream adoption. This book, Crypto Renaissance: Navigating the Bull Run of 2025, seeks to guide both new and seasoned investors through what promises to be one of the most transformative bull runs in the history of digital assets.

The story of cryptocurrency is one of constant change. From the early days of Bitcoin's launch in 2009 by the pseudonymous Satoshi Nakamoto, to the introduction of Ethereum in 2015, the market has undergone multiple phases of expansion, contraction, and innovation. Over the past decade, cryptocurrencies have matured into a multi-trillion-dollar industry. Yet, there are still many unanswered questions. How can we accurately predict the next phase of growth? What strategies should investors adopt to capitalize on the coming wave? And, most importantly, how can one successfully navigate a bull run in an asset class known for its extreme volatility?

In 2025, as we enter the next major bull cycle, these questions become more urgent than ever. The technological, financial, and regulatory landscapes are converging in such a way that the next bull run will likely be unlike any other. Institutional adoption is on the rise, with major corporations and financial institutions increasingly integrating cryptocurrency into their portfolios and services. At the same time, decentralized finance (DeFi) and blockchain-based innovations are reshaping the world of finance, allowing individuals greater control over their assets and creating new opportunities for wealth-building.

However, with these exciting developments comes a wave of uncertainty. Cryptocurrencies remain a high-risk, high-reward investment. Market corrections, scams, and the ever-changing regulatory landscape can create substantial risks for even the most experienced investors. Understanding these risks and knowing how to mitigate them is crucial to successfully navigating the bull run. This book will not only help you recognize the signs of a market surge but will also equip you with the tools and strategies to thrive during one of the most significant financial shifts of our time.

In this book, we will explore the fundamentals of cryptocurrency markets, the cycles that drive them, and how the bull run of 2025 is shaping up to be a turning point in the industry. We'll dive into the key players in the market, including Bitcoin, Ethereum, and other emerging cryptocurrencies. We will also examine the impact of institutional players, the rise of decentralized finance, and the role of regulation as we step into this new phase. Along the way, we'll provide practical strategies, risk management tips, and insights that will help you not only survive but thrive during the bull run of 2025 and beyond.

Whether you're an experienced investor or new to the world of cryptocurrency, this book is designed to give you a comprehensive roadmap for navigating the exciting and unpredictable journey ahead. The crypto renaissance is upon us, and it's time to prepare for one of the most exciting financial revolutions of the 21st century.

Chapter 1
Introduction to the Crypto Renaissance

The world of cryptocurrency has evolved dramatically since Bitcoin's humble beginnings in 2009. What started as a niche concept for tech enthusiasts and libertarians has rapidly transformed into a multi-trillion-dollar global industry. Over the years, the crypto ecosystem has expanded beyond just digital currencies to include innovative technologies such as blockchain, smart contracts, decentralized finance (DeFi), and non-fungible tokens (NFTs). As we approach 2025, many experts believe we are on the brink of a new phase in the crypto revolution — one that will significantly reshape the global financial landscape. This chapter delves into this transformation, which we call the Crypto Renaissance.

A renaissance, traditionally seen as a period of rebirth or revival, is the perfect metaphor for the next era in cryptocurrency. Just as the Renaissance period in history marked a revival of culture, learning, and artistic expression, the Crypto Renaissance represents a resurgence of innovation and adoption. It's a time when blockchain technology, once viewed as a mere tool for cryptocurrency, is now being harnessed for a wide range of applications, from supply chain management to healthcare and beyond. This technological renaissance is empowering new generations of entrepreneurs and developers to explore previously unimagined possibilities, propelling crypto into the mainstream.

For investors and market participants, the Crypto Renaissance signifies the convergence of factors that will propel the market to new heights. Key developments such as increased institutional adoption, the maturation of decentralized finance platforms, and the emergence of regulations that provide clarity to the market are all converging in 2025. This convergence has created the perfect storm for the next bull run, where crypto is poised to break through barriers and achieve unprecedented growth. In this chapter, we will explore the forces driving this transformation, offering insights into why 2025 is shaping up to be a landmark year in the world of cryptocurrency.

The Evolution of Cryptocurrency

Cryptocurrency, in its simplest form, is a type of digital currency that operates independently of a central authority, such as a government or financial institution. The concept of cryptocurrency, however, is far more complex and has evolved significantly since its inception. It all began with Bitcoin, which was introduced in 2009 by the mysterious figure Satoshi Nakamoto. Nakamoto's creation was revolutionary, offering a decentralized and secure method for transferring value over the internet without the need for intermediaries. Bitcoin was born out of a desire to create a peer-to-peer electronic cash system that could operate outside the reach of centralized financial systems, giving individuals more control over their money.

The early days of Bitcoin were marked by a small, tight-knit group of enthusiasts and developers experimenting with the technology. The first-ever transaction, often referred to as the "genesis block," involved Nakamoto sending 10 bitcoins to a developer named Hal Finney. At that time, Bitcoin had little to no value, with some early adopters mining coins simply for the sake of exploring the potential of this new digital asset. Bitcoin's value began to increase gradually in 2010 when the first recorded transaction occurred: someone paid 10,000 bitcoins for two pizzas. While this transaction would later become legendary due to the astronomical value of Bitcoin in later years, it was the first real-world use case that demonstrated the possibility of Bitcoin as a medium of exchange.

As Bitcoin gained popularity, the technology behind it—the blockchain—began to capture the interest of a broader audience. Blockchain is the underlying technology that enables the secure, decentralized transfer of digital assets. It is a public ledger that records all transactions across a network of computers, making it transparent and immutable. The concept of blockchain opened the door to a variety of potential applications beyond Bitcoin, leading to the development of new cryptocurrencies and decentralized systems. The next significant evolution came with the creation of Ethereum in 2015 by Vitalik Buterin, a programmer who saw the potential of blockchain technology to support applications beyond currency. Ethereum introduced the concept of "smart contracts," which are self-executing contracts with the terms of the agreement directly written into lines of code. This expanded the use of blockchain technology, allowing developers to build decentralized applications (DApps) on the Ethereum platform.

Ethereum's introduction of smart contracts was a game changer, giving birth to the decentralized finance (DeFi) ecosystem, which allows users to lend, borrow, and trade assets without relying on traditional financial intermediaries like banks. The rise of DeFi, along with other blockchain-based innovations such as NFTs (non-fungible tokens), signaled a major shift in how blockchain technology could be applied. NFTs, which became particularly popular in 2021, are unique digital assets that represent ownership of a specific item, such as art, music, or even virtual real estate. These developments expanded the possibilities of cryptocurrency and blockchain beyond simple transactions, leading to an explosion of new projects, tokens, and use cases.

Simultaneously, cryptocurrency started to gain more widespread recognition and acceptance. Initially viewed with skepticism by mainstream financial institutions, cryptocurrencies like Bitcoin and Ethereum began to attract the attention of institutional investors, corporations, and governments. Companies like Tesla and Square started to incorporate Bitcoin into their balance sheets, signaling a growing acceptance of cryptocurrency as a legitimate asset class. The rise of stablecoins—cryptocurrencies pegged to the value of traditional fiat currencies like the US dollar—further solidified the role of cryptocurrency in the global financial system. Stablecoins provide a bridge between the digital and traditional worlds, offering the benefits of cryptocurrency while reducing the volatility often associated with digital assets.

In recent years, cryptocurrencies have seen tremendous growth, both in terms of market capitalization and global adoption. As of 2025, the cryptocurrency market is valued at over $2 trillion, with thousands of different digital assets in circulation. The evolution of cryptocurrency from a niche technology to a global financial movement has been driven by technological advancements, increasing institutional adoption, and the emergence of new use cases. However, the journey is far from over. As we approach the Crypto Renaissance in 2025, the next phase of cryptocurrency's evolution promises to bring even more innovation, including advancements in blockchain scalability, privacy solutions, and regulatory clarity. The journey of cryptocurrency has only just begun, and the future is brimming with possibilities.

Why 2025 Marks a New Era

The year 2025 is poised to be a transformative year for the cryptocurrency industry, marking the beginning of a new era for digital assets. While cryptocurrencies have been around for over a decade, they have faced a series of challenges, from volatile market cycles to regulatory uncertainty. However, as we approach 2025, several key factors are converging to create a perfect storm of growth and innovation, making this year a critical moment in the evolution of digital assets. Institutional adoption, advancements in blockchain technology, clearer regulatory frameworks, and the rise of decentralized finance (DeFi) are all aligning to pave the way for cryptocurrency to achieve broader mainstream acceptance. These developments signal that 2025 will not only be a year of continued growth but also one that will redefine the role of cryptocurrencies in the global financial system.

The increasing involvement of institutional investors has played a significant role in setting the stage for this new era. In recent years, companies like Tesla, MicroStrategy, and Square have added Bitcoin to their balance sheets, signaling a shift from viewing cryptocurrencies as speculative assets to considering them as legitimate stores of value. This growing institutional interest is expected to accelerate in 2025 as more financial institutions integrate digital assets into their offerings. Banks and traditional financial services are slowly embracing blockchain and cryptocurrency technology, opening up new avenues for retail investors, corporations, and even governments to participate in the market. This shift will lead to further legitimacy for cryptocurrencies, which will continue to attract new investors and allow the industry to mature and stabilize. As the market becomes more structured and regulated, institutional investment is likely to drive a new wave of growth, making 2025 a banner year for digital assets.

Another key factor behind the new era of cryptocurrency is the ongoing evolution of blockchain technology. As blockchain networks such as Bitcoin and Ethereum continue to develop, they are becoming more scalable, secure, and energy-efficient. Ethereum's transition from proof-of-work to proof-of-stake with its Ethereum 2.0 upgrade will improve transaction speeds and reduce the network's environmental impact, addressing two of the major criticisms it has faced. In addition, new blockchain projects are focusing on solving scalability issues and increasing transaction throughput, allowing the entire ecosystem to handle higher volumes of transactions without compromising decentralization. These technological advancements will make cryptocurrencies more efficient and practical for everyday use, laying the foundation for greater adoption and a more stable market. The rise of decentralized finance (DeFi), enabled by smart contracts, is also pushing the boundaries of what blockchain technology can achieve, creating a decentralized alternative to traditional banking and finance that has the potential to disrupt the entire industry.

Finally, regulatory clarity is set to become a major milestone for the cryptocurrency market in 2025. While the regulatory landscape has been fragmented and often uncertain in the past, governments and regulators around the world are beginning to take more decisive actions. In countries like the United States, the European Union, and parts of Asia, clearer regulations are being introduced to provide a framework for the safe and transparent use of cryptocurrencies. These regulations will help protect investors from fraud and market manipulation, instill greater confidence in the industry, and allow for the further integration of cryptocurrencies into the global economy. By 2025, the clarity around cryptocurrency regulations will make it easier for businesses and investors to operate in the space, creating a more stable environment for the growth of the industry. As a result, the year 2025 is shaping up to be a turning point, not only in the growth of digital assets but also in their acceptance as a legitimate and vital part of the financial system.

In conclusion, 2025 marks a new era for cryptocurrency due to the convergence of several key trends: institutional adoption, technological advancements, and clearer regulations. These factors are driving the cryptocurrency industry toward greater maturity, legitimacy, and stability, setting the stage for even greater growth in the years to come. As we approach this pivotal year, cryptocurrency is no longer just a speculative investment but a powerful and transformative force that is reshaping the global financial landscape. For investors, developers, and innovators alike, the Crypto Renaissance of 2025 represents a unique opportunity to be part of one of the most significant economic shifts of our time.

The Impact of Blockchain Technology

Blockchain technology, the foundational framework behind cryptocurrencies like Bitcoin and Ethereum, has emerged as one of the most transformative innovations of the 21st century. At its core, blockchain is a decentralized, distributed ledger that records transactions across many computers in a way that ensures security, transparency, and immutability. While initially designed to support digital currencies, blockchain has far-reaching applications that extend well beyond the world of finance. Its ability to create trust, reduce reliance on intermediaries, and offer unprecedented levels of security has the potential to disrupt industries ranging from banking and insurance to healthcare, supply chain management, and even voting systems. The impact of blockchain technology is far-reaching, and as the technology continues to evolve, its influence will only grow in the coming years.

One of the most significant impacts of blockchain technology is the decentralization of control. Traditional financial systems and industries rely heavily on central authorities—such as banks, governments, and other intermediaries—to process transactions and validate information. This centralization creates points of failure, introduces inefficiencies, and often leads to trust issues between parties. Blockchain, on the other hand, operates without the need for a centralized authority. Transactions are validated by a network of nodes (computers) spread across the globe, and once a transaction is recorded on the blockchain, it cannot be altered. This decentralized approach reduces the risk of fraud, censorship, and manipulation, offering a more transparent and secure method of conducting business. As a result, industries that have traditionally relied on intermediaries are beginning to explore blockchain solutions that can streamline processes and improve transparency.

In addition to decentralization, blockchain provides a level of transparency that was previously unattainable in many industries. Each transaction on the blockchain is recorded on a public ledger, which can be accessed by anyone at any time. This openness ensures that all parties involved in a transaction can independently verify its legitimacy without needing to rely on a trusted third party. In sectors like supply chain management, for example, blockchain allows consumers to trace the origin of products, ensuring that goods are ethically sourced and produced. This level of transparency is also revolutionizing industries like finance, where the ability to audit transactions in real time can reduce instances of fraud and ensure regulatory compliance. With blockchain, there is no longer a need for trust in centralized institutions, as the technology itself guarantees the accuracy and authenticity of transactions.

Another critical impact of blockchain technology is its ability to enhance security. Traditional methods of securing data are often vulnerable to hacking, as they rely on centralized systems that can be breached. Blockchain technology, by contrast, uses encryption and consensus mechanisms to ensure the security of the information stored on the network. Once a transaction is added to the blockchain, it is nearly impossible to alter or reverse without the consensus of the network, making it extremely resistant to tampering or fraud. This level of security is particularly important in industries such as healthcare, where sensitive personal data needs to be protected from cyber threats. By utilizing blockchain, healthcare providers can create secure, immutable patient records that can be accessed only by authorized individuals, significantly reducing the risk of data breaches and identity theft. The same level of security can be applied to other industries, including finance, where blockchain can prevent fraudulent activities such as double-spending or unauthorized access to funds.

Blockchain's impact also extends to the world of smart contracts, which have the potential to automate and streamline various business processes. Smart contracts are self-executing contracts where the terms of the agreement are written into code and automatically executed when certain conditions are met. These contracts eliminate the need for intermediaries, such as lawyers or notaries, and ensure that all parties adhere to the terms of the agreement. For example, in the real estate industry, blockchain-based smart contracts can automatically transfer ownership of property once payment has been made, reducing the time and cost associated with traditional property transactions. In the world of finance, smart contracts can be used to facilitate automatic payments, settlement of trades, and even insurance claims, reducing administrative costs and increasing efficiency.

The adoption of blockchain technology is also transforming the concept of ownership. With blockchain, assets can be tokenized and securely traded on decentralized platforms. For example, non-fungible tokens (NFTs) represent unique digital assets that can be bought, sold, and traded. These tokens have opened up entirely new markets for art, music, and collectibles, providing artists and creators with a new way to monetize their work. Tokenization extends beyond digital assets to physical ones, allowing for fractional ownership of items such as real estate, artwork, or even shares in a business. This democratization of asset ownership has the potential to create more equitable financial systems and increase access to previously illiquid assets.

Finally, blockchain technology holds promise for creating more efficient and secure voting systems. Traditional voting methods, whether in elections or other decision-making processes, are often criticized for their vulnerability to fraud, tampering, or lack of transparency. Blockchain-based voting systems, however, offer a solution by creating immutable records of votes that are verified by multiple nodes in the network. This ensures that each vote is accurately counted, prevents tampering, and allows for real-time auditing. By providing a transparent, secure, and efficient method for voting, blockchain could help restore trust in democratic processes and reduce the risk of election fraud.

In conclusion, the impact of blockchain technology is profound and multifaceted. It has the potential to transform industries by enabling decentralization, enhancing transparency and security, and automating processes through smart contracts. As the technology continues to mature, we can expect even greater innovations that will further disrupt traditional systems and create new opportunities for businesses and individuals alike. Blockchain is not just a technological advancement; it is a paradigm shift that is reshaping the way we think about trust, security, and value in the digital age.

Chapter 2
Understanding Market Cycles

Cryptocurrency markets, much like any other financial markets, experience cyclical patterns of growth and contraction. These cycles, driven by a variety of factors such as investor sentiment, technological advancements, and macroeconomic conditions, play a significant role in determining the trajectory of prices over time. Understanding these market cycles is crucial for any investor, as it allows them to recognize the signs of market shifts, make informed decisions, and manage risks effectively. In this chapter, we will explore the various stages of a market cycle and how they apply to cryptocurrencies, providing you with the tools to navigate the volatility inherent in digital asset markets.

The concept of market cycles is not unique to cryptocurrencies. In traditional financial markets, cycles typically include periods of expansion, peak, contraction, and trough, known as the boom and bust cycle. In the world of cryptocurrencies, these phases are equally relevant but often occur with greater intensity due to the volatility and speculative nature of digital assets. Investors who can identify these phases early have a better chance of entering and exiting the market at optimal times, maximizing profits while minimizing the risks associated with market corrections. In this chapter, we will examine the factors that drive these cycles and how they can manifest in cryptocurrency markets, often with sharper price swings compared to traditional assets.

Cryptocurrency markets are also influenced by unique factors such as technological innovations, regulatory developments, and the increasing involvement of institutional investors. These variables can accelerate or dampen the progression of market cycles, making them more unpredictable but also offering new opportunities. Understanding how these factors interact with market psychology and investor behavior can provide valuable insights into predicting the next phase of a cycle. Whether you're a seasoned investor or just beginning your journey, recognizing the patterns within market cycles and their underlying drivers is a fundamental skill for navigating the often turbulent waters of cryptocurrency investing.

The Phases of a Bull Run

A bull run refers to a period in the market when prices of assets, such as cryptocurrencies, rise steadily and significantly over a prolonged period. These market phases, typically driven by investor sentiment, speculation, and fundamental growth, follow a predictable pattern. Understanding the phases of a bull run is essential for investors who aim to time their entries and exits effectively. The market does not rise in a straight line; rather, it moves through several distinct phases, each with unique characteristics, investor behaviors, and price movements. Recognizing these phases allows investors to adapt their strategies, capitalize on the opportunities each stage presents, and manage risks as the market progresses.

The first phase of a bull run is the accumulation phase, which typically occurs after a bear market or prolonged stagnation. In this phase, the market is still largely unaware of the upcoming rally. Prices are low, and the general sentiment is often bearish or uncertain. This is the phase where long-term, strategic investors begin to accumulate positions, often quietly and without drawing much attention. While the broader market remains skeptical, these investors recognize the value and potential of the asset, buying in as prices remain depressed. Accumulation is marked by low trading volume and subtle movements, with few investors realizing that the market is about to embark on an upward trajectory.

Once the initial accumulation takes place, the market enters the breakout phase. This is when prices begin to rise significantly, typically breaking through key resistance levels. As prices gain traction, more investors start to take notice, and media coverage begins to increase. The demand for the asset starts to build, and trading volumes rise as more participants begin entering the market. This phase is often characterized by a sense of cautious optimism, as prices move steadily upward. While the breakout marks the beginning of the bull run, there are still many skeptics, and the overall market sentiment can remain somewhat uncertain, especially in the early stages of the phase. It is during this time that some early investors, who have already accumulated positions, may begin to realize gains, but the market still has a significant amount of room to grow.

As the breakout phase progresses, the market enters what is known as the parabolic rise. This phase is marked by extreme growth, where prices rise at an accelerated rate, often with little regard for historical valuations or fundamentals. Investor enthusiasm reaches its peak during this phase, and the fear of missing out (FOMO) drives more participants to buy into the market, propelling prices even higher. The parabolic rise is typically a phase of heightened volatility, with prices surging to new highs in a relatively short period. Social media, news outlets, and online communities are buzzing with discussions about the asset, further fueling the buying frenzy.

However, as the market becomes overheated, the risk of a market correction grows. While the parabolic rise can offer substantial gains for those who time their entries well, it can also lead to significant losses for latecomers who buy at inflated prices, unaware that the market may be nearing its peak.

The final stages of a bull run often involve the peak and distribution phase. This is when prices reach their highest point, and the market begins to show signs of exhaustion. Investor sentiment is mixed, as some continue to buy in with the belief that the market will keep rising, while others begin to sell off their holdings, capitalizing on their gains. The distribution phase is marked by high volatility, with large price swings as investors take profits. The selling pressure from early investors who have seen substantial returns can cause the market to stall or even experience brief corrections. At this point, the market is typically overextended, and while there is still some optimism, the risks of a downturn become more apparent. As the bull run reaches its peak, the balance of buyers and sellers shifts, and the market prepares for the inevitable correction or bear market.

In conclusion, the phases of a bull run are marked by distinct shifts in market behavior and sentiment. From the quiet accumulation of undervalued assets to the explosive price increases of the parabolic rise, each phase offers unique opportunities and risks. By understanding the characteristics of each phase, investors can better navigate the market, positioning themselves to profit during periods of growth and minimize losses when the market eventually corrects. The key to successful participation in a bull run lies in timing, discipline, and a clear understanding of market dynamics.

Identifying Market Trends

Identifying market trends is a fundamental skill for any investor, particularly in the highly volatile world of cryptocurrencies. Market trends represent the general direction in which an asset or the market as a whole is moving over a period of time. Recognizing these trends early can offer significant opportunities to capitalize on price movements, while failing to do so can result in missed opportunities or substantial losses. In the world of cryptocurrency, where market fluctuations are often rapid and unpredictable, understanding how to identify and interpret market trends is crucial for making informed investment decisions.

Market trends typically fall into three main categories: uptrends, downtrends, and sideways trends. An uptrend occurs when the price of an asset consistently rises over time, forming a series of higher highs and higher lows. This is typically a sign of increasing demand and investor confidence. Conversely, a downtrend is characterized by a series of lower highs and lower lows, indicating that selling pressure is outweighing buying demand. Sideways trends, or ranging markets, occur when the price fluctuates within a certain range, neither moving significantly upward nor downward. These trends indicate indecision in the market and are often seen during periods of consolidation or before a significant breakout or breakdown.

The ability to recognize these trends requires a solid understanding of technical analysis, which involves studying historical price data and using various indicators to predict future price movements. One of the most fundamental tools for identifying trends is the use of trendlines. Trendlines are drawn on price charts to visually represent the direction of price movement. In an uptrend, a trendline is drawn by connecting the lows of the price action, while in a downtrend, the trendline is drawn by connecting the highs. A trend is considered valid as long as the price remains above the trendline in an uptrend or below it in a downtrend. A break in the trendline can signal a potential reversal, prompting traders to adjust their strategies.

Another important tool for identifying trends is moving averages. A moving average smooths out price data over a set period, helping to filter out short-term fluctuations and reveal the underlying direction of the market. The two most commonly used types of moving averages are the simple moving average (SMA) and the exponential moving average (EMA). The moving average can help traders identify whether an asset is in an uptrend, downtrend, or sideways trend. For example, when the price is consistently above the moving average, it signals an uptrend, while being below the moving average indicates a downtrend. Crossovers between short-term and long-term moving averages are also important indicators of potential trend reversals. When a short-term moving average crosses above a long-term moving average, it is considered a bullish signal, and when it crosses below, it is seen as a bearish signal.

Volume is another critical factor in identifying market trends. Volume refers to the number of assets traded over a specific period and can be an important indicator of the strength or weakness of a trend. When an asset is in an uptrend, increasing volume typically confirms the strength of the trend, as it indicates growing interest and participation in the market. Conversely, a decrease in volume during an uptrend can signal that the trend is losing momentum. Similarly, during a downtrend, rising volume can indicate strong selling pressure, while declining volume may suggest that the trend is nearing its end.

The Relative Strength Index (RSI) is another popular tool for identifying market trends, particularly for gauging whether an asset is overbought or oversold. The RSI measures the speed and change of price movements, ranging from 0 to 100. An RSI above 70 indicates that an asset may be overbought and due for a correction, while an RSI below 30 suggests that it may be oversold and could be poised for a rebound. By analyzing the RSI in conjunction with price trends, investors can gain valuable insights into the strength of the prevailing trend.

Chart patterns also play a crucial role in identifying market trends. Common patterns such as head and shoulders, double tops, and double bottoms can signal trend reversals, while continuation patterns like triangles, flags, and pennants indicate that the prevailing trend is likely to continue. These patterns provide traders with valuable clues about the market's direction and help them make more informed predictions about future price movements.

Sentiment analysis is another important aspect of identifying market trends, particularly in the cryptocurrency space, where investor sentiment can be highly volatile and driven by news, social media, and external events. Monitoring sentiment through social media platforms, news sources, and specialized sentiment analysis tools can help investors gauge the overall mood of the market and anticipate potential trend shifts. For instance, if there is widespread positive sentiment surrounding a particular cryptocurrency due to a major technological development or positive news, it may indicate that an uptrend is about to begin. Conversely, negative news or a shift in sentiment could signal the start of a downtrend.

In conclusion, identifying market trends is a key skill for cryptocurrency investors and traders. By combining technical analysis, chart patterns, volume analysis, and sentiment indicators, investors can better understand the market's direction and make more informed decisions. While no method can guarantee perfect accuracy in predicting future price movements, recognizing and responding to market trends in a timely manner can help investors maximize their profits and minimize their risks in the volatile cryptocurrency markets. The ability to identify and adapt to changing market trends is essential for navigating the fast-paced world of digital assets successfully.

Lessons from Previous Bull Runs

Cryptocurrency markets are known for their extreme volatility, and previous bull runs have provided investors with valuable lessons on navigating such unpredictable cycles. One of the most crucial takeaways from past bull runs is the importance of timing. The cryptocurrency market tends to attract a lot of excitement during these periods, and many retail investors jump in as prices rise, hoping to catch the wave of growth. However, many of these investors enter the market too late, after prices have already surged significantly. By the time they decide to buy in, they often end up purchasing at the peak, just before the market corrects. Timing is essential, and those who enter the market early during accumulation or breakout phases have a better chance of profiting than those who join in at the peak. Successful investors are those who understand market cycles, wait for the right moment, and make informed decisions rather than following the herd when the market is overheated.

Another lesson from previous bull runs is the necessity of volatility and risk management. Cryptocurrencies are inherently volatile, with prices often increasing rapidly during a bull run, followed by sharp declines. For example, during Bitcoin's 2017 bull run, the price skyrocketed from around $1,000 at the start of the year to nearly $20,000 by December, only to plummet back down to around $3,000 the following year. This kind of volatility can be emotionally taxing for investors who are unprepared for the market's swings. Risk management strategies such as setting stop-loss orders, diversifying portfolios, and not investing more than one can afford to lose are essential for surviving a bull run. It's important to remember that while there are substantial gains to be made, the volatility of the market also means there are risks involved, and protecting oneself from large losses is just as important as capitalizing on the upside.

Market sentiment also plays a key role in driving bull runs and can be both a blessing and a curse for investors. During bull runs, positive sentiment spreads like wildfire, often amplified by social media and news coverage. As prices rise, more and more investors pile in, driven by the fear of missing out (FOMO), and the cycle continues to feed itself. However, this psychological phenomenon can lead to unsustainable price increases, driven more by hype than by solid fundamentals. This is a critical lesson from past bull runs—investors should be cautious of getting swept up in the euphoria and should avoid making decisions based solely on sentiment. Just as quickly as the market can rise, it can also fall once sentiment turns negative. The 2017 bull run serves as a reminder that when sentiment shifts, prices can drop rapidly, catching latecomers off guard and leaving them with significant losses.

Overvaluation is another key issue that has plagued many investors in past bull runs. When prices rise too quickly and without justification, assets can become overvalued. The 2017 Bitcoin surge saw prices skyrocket to levels that could not be justified by the fundamentals at the time. Investors, caught up in the speculative frenzy, often ignored the long-term viability of the asset and made decisions based on short-term price movements. This resulted in substantial corrections after the bubble burst. The lesson here is that investors should be mindful of overvaluation and avoid basing their decisions solely on price trends. Understanding the intrinsic value of an asset, particularly when it comes to technological developments, adoption rates, and market demand, is essential for making sound investment choices in a bull run.

Finally, patience is a virtue that previous bull runs have taught investors. While it's tempting to chase quick profits in a rising market, successful investors understand that long-term growth requires time and careful decision-making. The 2017 bull run, followed by its dramatic crash, proved that cryptocurrency markets need time to reset. After such dramatic surges and corrections, the market often enters a consolidation phase, and it can take months or even years for prices to stabilize before another bull run begins. Patience during these periods is crucial, as it allows investors to avoid panic selling and to make informed decisions based on market fundamentals rather than short-term fluctuations. Cryptocurrency investing should be viewed with a long-term mindset, and successful investors understand that the market moves in cycles that require resilience and patience to navigate.

In conclusion, the lessons learned from previous bull runs emphasize the need for strategic thinking and a disciplined approach to investing. Timing the market, managing risk, understanding market sentiment, being cautious of overvaluation, and maintaining patience are all crucial elements of a successful investment strategy. By reflecting on past market cycles and applying these lessons, investors can better position themselves to make informed decisions and navigate future bull runs with greater confidence and success. The volatile nature of cryptocurrency markets means that there will always be risks, but with careful planning and a long-term perspective, these risks can be mitigated, allowing investors to capitalize on the opportunities that arise.

Chapter 3
Preparing for the Bull Run

As the cryptocurrency market enters a new phase of growth, the ability to prepare for a bull run becomes a crucial aspect of a successful investment strategy. Bull runs, though exciting and full of opportunity, can also be highly volatile and unpredictable, making preparation essential for both seasoned and new investors alike. A key to thriving in these periods of rapid price increases lies in laying the groundwork beforehand. By understanding market cycles, identifying early signs of an impending bull run, and having a clear plan in place, investors can position themselves to take full advantage of the opportunities presented during these times of growth.

Preparation for a bull run starts with building a strong foundation. Before diving into any market, it's essential to have a clear understanding of risk management, diversification, and overall investment goals. A well-thought-out strategy should include setting realistic expectations, determining how much capital you are willing to invest, and knowing your risk tolerance. During a bull run, emotions such as greed and FOMO (fear of missing out) can cloud judgment, leading investors to make rash decisions. Having a predefined plan for entering and exiting the market, coupled with strategies like setting stop-loss orders and taking profits at key milestones, ensures that you remain disciplined even when market euphoria peaks. This preparation will help you manage risks effectively and make more calculated, informed decisions during the excitement of a bull run.

Another critical aspect of preparing for a bull run is conducting thorough research into the assets you plan to invest in. While Bitcoin and Ethereum remain the most prominent cryptocurrencies, emerging altcoins and DeFi projects also offer significant potential for growth. Identifying promising assets early, before they enter the mainstream spotlight, can lead to considerable gains during a bull run. Understanding the underlying technology, the team behind a project, and the use case of the token or coin are all essential elements that should guide your investment decisions. Additionally, keeping an eye on news, market sentiment, and any regulatory developments will allow you to adjust your strategy accordingly as the market evolves. By preparing in advance and staying informed, you can position yourself to capitalize on the opportunities that a bull run brings while minimizing unnecessary risks.

Building a Solid Foundation: Risk Management

Risk management is a cornerstone of successful investing, particularly in the cryptocurrency market, which is renowned for its volatility. The potential for high returns in cryptocurrency can often cloud the inherent risks, leading investors to take positions without adequately considering the potential downside. Building a solid foundation for any investment strategy starts with establishing a clear approach to risk management, ensuring that investors are not only positioned to capitalize on potential gains but also protected from significant losses. Effective risk management involves assessing, mitigating, and controlling the risks associated with market fluctuations, all while keeping long-term goals in mind.

The first step in risk management is determining your risk tolerance. Risk tolerance is the amount of risk you are willing to take on based on your financial situation, investment goals, and personal comfort with volatility. Since cryptocurrencies can experience drastic price swings, understanding how much risk you can tolerate without compromising your peace of mind or financial stability is essential. To gauge your risk tolerance, consider factors such as your investment horizon, financial goals, and the amount of capital you can afford to lose. For example, an investor nearing retirement might have a low risk tolerance, preferring to allocate a larger portion of their portfolio to stable, low-risk assets. In contrast, younger investors with a longer investment horizon may be more willing to take on higher levels of risk for the potential of greater returns. Once you understand your risk tolerance, you can tailor your investment strategy to match, ensuring that you remain comfortable with your decisions, even when the market fluctuates.

Once risk tolerance is established, diversification becomes a key element of any solid risk management strategy. In the world of cryptocurrency, diversification involves spreading your investments across different assets, such as Bitcoin, Ethereum, and a range of altcoins or tokens. This approach helps reduce the impact of any single asset's poor performance on your overall portfolio. Cryptocurrencies, like other asset classes, can experience periods of extreme volatility, and holding a diversified portfolio helps smooth out the ups and downs. For example, if Bitcoin experiences a significant drop in value, other assets in your portfolio, particularly those that may not be as correlated with Bitcoin, can help cushion the blow. In addition to spreading investments across different cryptocurrencies, diversification can also extend to other asset classes like stocks, bonds, or real estate. By diversifying, you are less exposed to the risks associated with any one asset and can take advantage of opportunities across different markets and industries.

Another crucial aspect of risk management is setting stop-loss orders. A stop-loss order is an automatic order to sell an asset once it reaches a specific price, helping to limit potential losses. In a highly volatile market like cryptocurrency, prices can swing dramatically within short periods, and stop-loss orders help protect investors from large losses during these fluctuations. Setting stop-loss levels requires thoughtful consideration and knowledge of the market's behavior. Too tight of a stop-loss can trigger a sell order too early during temporary price fluctuations, potentially locking in losses before the market has had time to recover. On the other hand, setting the stop-loss too wide may expose an investor to larger losses if the market continues to decline. The key is to set stop-loss levels that reflect a reasonable level of risk while still allowing for the natural fluctuations that occur in the crypto market. Many investors set stop-loss orders based on percentage drops, such as 5%, 10%, or 20%, depending on their risk tolerance and the volatility of the asset they hold.

In addition to stop-loss orders, regularly reviewing and adjusting your portfolio is essential to effective risk management. As the cryptocurrency market is dynamic, with new developments, technologies, and regulatory changes occurring frequently, it is important to periodically reassess your investments. This review process involves looking at the performance of your assets, analyzing market trends, and determining whether adjustments need to be made to your portfolio. For instance, if a particular asset is underperforming or the market conditions change, it may be wise to rebalance your portfolio by reallocating funds to more promising investments. Similarly, if an asset becomes too large a portion of your portfolio due to its price increase, you may want to trim back your position to maintain a balanced risk exposure.

Finally, managing risk also means managing emotions. Cryptocurrency markets are often driven by euphoria during bull runs and fear during downturns. This emotional volatility can cloud judgment and lead to poor decision-making. Investors may be tempted to hold onto an asset for too long during a bull run, hoping for more profits, or they may panic-sell during a correction or bear market. One of the most important components of risk management is the ability to remain level-headed, stick to your strategy, and avoid making decisions driven by short-term emotions. Developing a disciplined approach to investing, including setting predetermined entry and exit points, can help investors avoid making impulsive decisions based on market noise.

In conclusion, building a solid foundation for cryptocurrency investing begins with a thoughtful and disciplined approach to risk management. Understanding your risk tolerance, diversifying your investments, setting stop-loss orders, regularly reviewing your portfolio, and managing emotions are all essential components of a strong risk management strategy. By incorporating these practices into your investing approach, you not only increase your chances of success but also ensure that you can withstand the inevitable volatility that comes with cryptocurrency markets. The goal is not just to make profitable investments but to protect your capital and manage risk in a way that aligns with your long-term financial objectives.

The Role of Technical Analysis

Technical analysis plays a central role in the world of cryptocurrency investing, providing investors and traders with tools to predict future price movements based on past market data. Unlike fundamental analysis, which evaluates the intrinsic value of an asset based on factors like technology, adoption, and governance, technical analysis focuses solely on price, volume, and chart patterns. By studying historical data and using various indicators, technical analysis helps market participants make more informed decisions, understand market trends, and identify entry and exit points. In the volatile and fast-paced cryptocurrency market, technical analysis is an invaluable tool for navigating price fluctuations and making strategic moves.

At the core of technical analysis is the belief that all information relevant to a financial asset, including market sentiment, is reflected in its price. This principle suggests that by analyzing price charts, traders can uncover patterns that have historically indicated certain market behaviors, such as price movements or reversals. The main goal of technical analysis is to predict future price trends, which can then inform investment decisions. For instance, if a cryptocurrency's price shows a consistent upward movement, technical analysts may predict that the trend will continue, encouraging investors to enter the market or hold their positions. Conversely, if a downward trend is identified, traders may choose to sell or avoid investing in the asset.

One of the most widely used tools in technical analysis is price charts, which graphically display the historical price movements of an asset. These charts are essential for identifying trends, patterns, and key support and resistance levels. The most common chart types include line charts, bar charts, and candlestick charts, with candlestick charts being particularly popular in cryptocurrency markets. Each candlestick represents a specific time period (such as one minute, one hour, or one day) and displays the open, high, low, and close prices for that period. By analyzing the patterns created by these candlesticks, traders can identify potential market reversals or continuation patterns. For example, the appearance of a "bullish engulfing" candlestick pattern may signal the beginning of an upward trend, while a "bearish engulfing" pattern could indicate a potential reversal to the downside.

In addition to chart patterns, technical analysts use a variety of indicators and oscillators to assess market conditions and predict future price movements. Moving averages, for example, are one of the most common and versatile indicators used in technical analysis. A moving average is calculated by averaging the price of an asset over a specified period, helping to smooth out short-term price fluctuations and highlight longer-term trends. The two most commonly used types of moving averages are the Simple Moving Average (SMA) and the Exponential Moving Average (EMA). When the price is above the moving average, it indicates an uptrend, and when it is below, it signals a downtrend. Moving average crossovers, where a short-term moving average crosses above a long-term moving average, can also serve as buy signals, while the reverse crossover may signal a sell opportunity.

Another essential tool for technical analysis is the Relative Strength Index (RSI), an oscillator that measures the speed and change of price movements. The RSI is used to identify whether an asset is overbought or oversold, which can provide valuable insights into potential market reversals. The RSI ranges from 0 to 100, with readings above 70 typically indicating that an asset is overbought, and readings below 30 suggesting that it is oversold. By using the RSI in conjunction with other indicators, traders can confirm potential buy or sell signals and avoid making decisions based solely on a single indicator.

Volume is another crucial element in technical analysis. Volume refers to the number of shares or contracts traded during a given time period, and it provides insight into the strength or weakness of a price move. A price increase accompanied by high volume suggests that the trend is strong and likely to continue, while a price increase with low volume may signal that the trend is not sustainable and could reverse. Similarly, a price drop with high volume could indicate that selling pressure is significant, whereas a decline with low volume may suggest that the market is simply consolidating or preparing for a reversal.

Support and resistance levels are also key concepts in technical analysis. Support refers to a price level where an asset tends to find buying interest, preventing the price from falling further. Resistance, on the other hand, is a price level where selling pressure tends to emerge, capping the asset's upward movement. By identifying key support and resistance levels on a price chart, traders can predict potential breakout or breakdown points and plan their entries and exits accordingly. These levels are often used to set stop-loss orders, limit orders, or to gauge whether the market is likely to reverse or continue its trend.

Technical analysis is not foolproof, and it does have its limitations, especially in the unpredictable world of cryptocurrency. The market can be influenced by factors such as sudden regulatory changes, news events, or technological developments that are not reflected in historical price data. As such, technical analysis should be used in conjunction with other methods of analysis, such as fundamental analysis and market sentiment, to form a more complete understanding of the market.

In conclusion, technical analysis is an essential tool for cryptocurrency investors and traders, providing them with a framework for understanding market behavior and predicting price movements. By using price charts, indicators, and other analytical tools, traders can identify trends, spot potential market reversals, and make more informed decisions about when to buy or sell. While technical analysis is not a guaranteed method for success, it is a powerful approach that, when used correctly and in conjunction with other strategies, can help investors navigate the complexities of the cryptocurrency market with greater confidence and precision.

Developing a Winning Strategy

Developing a winning strategy is the cornerstone of success in the cryptocurrency market, where volatility and unpredictability are the norm. Given the unique nature of the crypto space, a well-crafted strategy is essential for managing risks, capitalizing on opportunities, and navigating the market's cyclical movements. Whether you're a long-term investor or a short-term trader, having a clear and actionable plan can help you achieve your financial goals while minimizing the emotional rollercoaster that often accompanies cryptocurrency investing.

The first step in developing a winning strategy is to define your investment goals. Before diving into the market, it's important to understand your objectives and the role that cryptocurrencies will play in your overall portfolio. Are you looking for long-term wealth accumulation, or are you interested in taking advantage of short-term price swings? Your goals will determine the type of strategy you should adopt. Long-term investors may focus on holding strong, well-established cryptocurrencies like Bitcoin and Ethereum, while short-term traders may seek to profit from rapid price movements in smaller altcoins. Defining your goals not only helps you decide which assets to invest in but also guides you in determining your risk tolerance and time horizon.

Once your goals are established, the next step is to assess your risk tolerance. Cryptocurrency markets are inherently volatile, with prices capable of moving by double-digit percentages in a single day. As such, determining how much risk you are willing to take on is essential for developing a strategy that aligns with your comfort level and financial capacity. If you are risk-averse, you might allocate your portfolio toward more stable, large-cap cryptocurrencies and use risk management techniques such as setting stop-loss orders. On the other hand, if you are comfortable with higher risk, you may choose to invest in smaller, emerging projects with the potential for high returns, albeit with the possibility of greater losses. Understanding your risk tolerance helps you to determine the size of each investment and decide whether you should diversify your holdings to spread risk.

Diversification is another key component of a winning strategy. The cryptocurrency market is filled with thousands of different coins and tokens, each with unique use cases and varying levels of volatility. By diversifying your portfolio, you reduce the risk of a single asset's poor performance severely affecting your overall investment. A diversified portfolio can include a mix of established assets like Bitcoin and Ethereum, along with promising altcoins or DeFi tokens that may offer higher growth potential. Additionally, diversification can extend beyond cryptocurrency, including traditional asset classes such as stocks, bonds, and real estate. This broader diversification ensures that your portfolio isn't overly reliant on the unpredictable nature of the crypto market, making it easier to weather downturns or corrections.

Another important element of a successful strategy is adopting a disciplined approach to entry and exit points. Timing the market can be extremely difficult, but by establishing clear criteria for when to buy or sell, you can avoid emotional decision-making during periods of market volatility. Many investors use technical analysis, such as identifying support and resistance levels, moving averages, and chart patterns, to determine optimal entry and exit points. Setting specific price targets for buying and selling based on these technical indicators can help you avoid getting caught up in the hype or fear of missing out (FOMO) during market rallies. Furthermore, establishing stop-loss orders at predetermined levels can protect you from significant losses during market downturns, ensuring that your downside risk is limited.

In addition to technical analysis, market sentiment plays a critical role in the development of a successful strategy. Cryptocurrency markets are heavily influenced by sentiment, with price movements often driven by news, social media, and broader market trends. Understanding the psychology of the market and recognizing when fear or greed is taking control can help you make more rational decisions. It's important to remember that market sentiment can often be short-lived, and prices can reverse quickly. A strategy that incorporates sentiment analysis, along with a focus on fundamentals and technical indicators, can provide a more holistic approach to identifying entry and exit points. Staying up to date on news and developments in the crypto space, such as regulatory changes, technological advancements, and major partnerships, can help you anticipate market movements and adjust your strategy accordingly.

Lastly, one of the most critical aspects of any winning strategy is continuous learning and adaptation. The cryptocurrency market is dynamic and constantly evolving, and what works today may not work tomorrow. By staying informed, attending webinars, reading books, and learning from other successful traders, you can refine your strategy over time. It's important to track your performance, review your past decisions, and learn from both your successes and mistakes. Many successful investors and traders develop their strategies through trial and error, constantly fine-tuning their approach to stay ahead of market trends.

In conclusion, developing a winning strategy in cryptocurrency requires a well-rounded approach that includes setting clear goals, assessing risk tolerance, diversifying your portfolio, using technical analysis, understanding market sentiment, and continuously learning. A disciplined, strategic approach helps you avoid emotional decision-making and better position yourself for success in a market known for its unpredictability. While no strategy guarantees success, those who develop a thoughtful plan and stick to it, adjusting as needed based on market conditions, are far more likely to achieve long-term profitability.

Chapter 4
The Role of Institutional Investors

The involvement of institutional investors in the cryptocurrency market has become one of the most significant factors influencing its growth and development. Historically, cryptocurrencies were seen as a niche market, primarily populated by individual retail investors and driven by the enthusiasm of early adopters. However, over the past few years, institutional players—such as hedge funds, investment firms, asset managers, and even large corporations—have begun to take a more prominent role. Their entry has not only brought significant capital inflows into the market but has also contributed to its maturation and increased legitimacy. In this chapter, we will explore how institutional investors are shaping the cryptocurrency landscape and what their growing influence means for both the market and individual investors.

Institutional investors bring several advantages to the cryptocurrency market, one of the most notable being liquidity. The participation of large financial institutions has added billions of dollars in capital, making it easier for both retail and institutional investors to buy and sell cryptocurrencies without significantly affecting market prices. This liquidity is vital for the long-term sustainability of the market, as it reduces the volatility that often characterizes cryptocurrency assets. Furthermore, institutional involvement has also led to the development of new financial products, such as cryptocurrency ETFs, futures, and options, which make it easier for institutional investors to gain exposure to digital assets. These financial products have helped to bridge the gap between traditional finance and the crypto space, opening up new avenues for investment and further legitimizing digital currencies in the eyes of the mainstream financial sector.

While the capital and liquidity that institutional investors bring to the market are undoubtedly beneficial, their presence also introduces new dynamics that can influence market behavior. Institutional investors tend to have longer investment horizons and more sophisticated strategies than retail investors, often focusing on factors such as fundamental analysis and long-term growth potential. As a result, their entry into the market can bring more stability and less speculative behavior, helping to smooth out the extreme price fluctuations that are common in crypto markets. However, their larger-scale movements can also lead to significant price swings when they decide to enter or exit positions. Understanding the role of institutional investors is therefore essential for anyone looking to navigate the evolving cryptocurrency market, as their influence continues to grow and shape the future of digital assets.

Mainstream Adoption of Crypto

The mainstream adoption of cryptocurrency represents a transformative shift in the financial world, as digital assets move from a niche, speculative investment to a widely accepted and integrated part of the global economy. Over the past decade, cryptocurrencies like Bitcoin and Ethereum have evolved from being largely experimental to being regarded as legitimate forms of investment, and even as a potential medium of exchange for goods and services.

This transition has been driven by a combination of technological advancements, regulatory clarity, institutional interest, and growing public awareness. The mainstreaming of crypto is not just about more people buying and selling digital currencies; it encompasses their use in various industries, integration with traditional financial systems, and recognition by governments and corporations as valuable assets.

A key factor in the mainstream adoption of cryptocurrencies is the increasing recognition of blockchain technology's potential beyond just financial transactions. Blockchain, the decentralized ledger technology that underpins cryptocurrencies, has proven to be valuable in numerous sectors, including supply chain management, healthcare, and real estate. Its ability to provide secure, transparent, and immutable records has caught the attention of various industries looking to streamline processes and reduce fraud. As blockchain technology becomes more widely used, cryptocurrencies gain legitimacy by association. This broader acceptance of blockchain has paved the way for cryptocurrencies to be considered not only as digital assets but as essential components of an evolving technological ecosystem that is reshaping traditional business practices.

The involvement of institutional investors has also played a crucial role in accelerating the adoption of cryptocurrencies. Once viewed with skepticism by major financial institutions, digital currencies have begun to attract interest from hedge funds, asset managers, and even traditional banks. Institutional investors bring significant capital to the market, contributing to the growth of the entire crypto ecosystem. Companies like Tesla and Square have publicly announced Bitcoin purchases, while major financial institutions such as JPMorgan and Goldman Sachs have begun offering cryptocurrency-related products to their clients. The introduction of crypto exchange-traded funds (ETFs) and Bitcoin futures contracts has further integrated cryptocurrencies into traditional financial markets, providing investors with more access points to crypto assets. This institutional interest not only increases liquidity in the market but also signals to the wider public that cryptocurrencies are no longer a fringe asset class but a legitimate part of the financial world.

Government regulation has also been a crucial factor in the mainstream adoption of cryptocurrencies. Over the years, many countries have moved from a stance of uncertainty or outright prohibition to developing more comprehensive regulatory frameworks. This shift has provided more clarity for investors, businesses, and consumers, reducing the risks associated with regulatory changes or potential crackdowns. In countries like the United States, the European Union, and Japan, governments are increasingly creating rules to govern cryptocurrency exchanges, protect consumers, and prevent money laundering or other illicit activities. These regulations help establish a framework that fosters trust in the cryptocurrency space, making it more attractive to institutional investors and the general public. Countries like El Salvador have even gone as far as adopting Bitcoin as legal tender, which marks a significant milestone in the mainstream acceptance of cryptocurrency as a legitimate currency.

Alongside regulatory progress, the technological advancements in cryptocurrency infrastructure have made it easier for the general public to access and use digital currencies. Cryptocurrency exchanges, which were once difficult to navigate, have become more user-friendly, offering intuitive interfaces for both beginners and experienced traders. Wallets and payment solutions that allow consumers to hold and spend cryptocurrencies have become more secure and easier to use. The rise of stablecoins, which are pegged to traditional fiat currencies like the US dollar, has also provided a less volatile entry point for people looking to engage with cryptocurrencies without the fear of drastic price fluctuations. As cryptocurrencies become more accessible to a wider range of people, the barriers to entry continue to decrease, further accelerating their adoption.

Furthermore, the increasing use of cryptocurrencies in real-world applications, such as online purchases, remittances, and decentralized finance (DeFi), is solidifying their position in the mainstream. Large companies like Microsoft, Overstock, and Newegg accept Bitcoin as payment for goods and services, signaling the growing recognition of crypto as a viable payment method. Cryptocurrency's role in remittances, particularly in countries with unstable currencies or high transaction fees, has become an essential use case, enabling individuals to send money across borders quickly and cheaply. The rise of decentralized finance platforms, which leverage blockchain and cryptocurrency to offer services like lending, borrowing, and trading without the need for traditional banks, is also contributing to the mainstream adoption of crypto. DeFi platforms have seen massive growth, providing a decentralized alternative to traditional financial institutions and democratizing access to financial services.

The mainstream adoption of cryptocurrencies is also being fueled by growing public awareness and education. As cryptocurrencies gain more attention in the media, people are becoming more curious about how they work and their potential benefits. Educational initiatives, online communities, and influencers have played a role in demystifying cryptocurrencies and blockchain technology for the public. As the understanding of digital assets increases, more individuals are willing to explore them as an investment or even as part of their daily lives.

In conclusion, the mainstream adoption of cryptocurrency is a multifaceted process that involves the acceptance and integration of digital assets into various industries, financial systems, and government frameworks. Institutional involvement, regulatory clarity, technological advancements, and real-world use cases have all contributed to the growing legitimacy and acceptance of cryptocurrencies. As the landscape continues to evolve, it is likely that cryptocurrencies will become an increasingly integral part of the global financial system, offering new opportunities for investment, financial inclusion, and technological innovation. The future of cryptocurrencies is promising, and their mainstream adoption is expected to continue shaping the financial world in the years to come.

Institutional Investment Vehicles

Institutional investment vehicles are specialized financial instruments designed for large investors, such as pension funds, hedge funds, insurance companies, and other institutional investors, to gain exposure to various asset classes, including cryptocurrencies. These vehicles provide an essential bridge between traditional financial markets and the emerging cryptocurrency space. Institutional investors, due to their size and regulatory requirements, cannot typically purchase assets like Bitcoin or Ethereum directly from exchanges in the same way retail investors can. Instead, they utilize institutional investment vehicles, which offer a more secure, compliant, and efficient means of gaining exposure to digital assets. The rise of these vehicles has been a significant factor in the mainstream adoption of cryptocurrencies, as they make it easier for large investors to incorporate digital assets into their portfolios while mitigating risks related to liquidity, custody, and regulatory compliance.

One of the most common institutional investment vehicles for cryptocurrencies is the **Bitcoin Futures contract**. A futures contract is a standardized agreement to buy or sell an asset at a predetermined price at a specified time in the future. Bitcoin Futures allow institutional investors to gain exposure to the price of Bitcoin without having to actually buy and hold the cryptocurrency itself. Bitcoin Futures contracts are primarily traded on regulated exchanges like the Chicago Mercantile Exchange (CME) and the Chicago Board Options Exchange (CBOE). These contracts provide investors with a way to speculate on the price of Bitcoin or hedge against Bitcoin price fluctuations, without the complexities and risks associated with owning the asset directly. The approval of Bitcoin Futures by regulatory authorities like the U.S. Commodity Futures Trading Commission (CFTC) has provided institutional investors with greater confidence in entering the cryptocurrency space.

Another prominent institutional investment vehicle is the **Bitcoin Exchange-Traded Fund (ETF)**. A Bitcoin ETF is a fund that tracks the price of Bitcoin and is traded on traditional stock exchanges, similar to other exchange-traded funds. A Bitcoin ETF provides institutional investors with exposure to Bitcoin through a highly liquid, regulated investment vehicle. The ETF structure allows investors to gain indirect exposure to Bitcoin's price movements, without needing to worry about managing private keys or securely storing the cryptocurrency. Bitcoin ETFs are appealing to institutional investors because they fit easily within existing investment portfolios, providing tax efficiency, and they comply with existing securities regulations. In recent years, Bitcoin ETFs have become increasingly popular, with several proposals under review by regulatory bodies like the U.S. Securities and Exchange Commission (SEC), marking a step forward in bringing Bitcoin into mainstream institutional investing.

Beyond Bitcoin Futures and ETFs, there are other forms of institutional investment vehicles for cryptocurrencies, including **Grayscale Bitcoin Trust (GBTC)** and **crypto-focused hedge funds**. The Grayscale Bitcoin Trust is one of the most well-known and accessible ways for institutional investors to gain exposure to Bitcoin. GBTC is a publicly traded trust that holds Bitcoin on behalf of its investors. The trust shares trade on over-the-counter (OTC) markets, and each share represents a fraction of Bitcoin held by the trust. The advantage of GBTC is that it allows investors to gain exposure to Bitcoin without directly owning the asset, providing a regulated and easy-to-access vehicle. It also offers the benefits of traditional securities, such as the ability to hold shares in tax-advantaged accounts like IRAs. However, GBTC shares often trade at a premium or discount to the actual value of the Bitcoin held in the trust, which can create pricing inefficiencies.

Crypto-focused hedge funds are another growing segment of institutional investment vehicles. These funds pool capital from institutional investors and employ various strategies, including long-only, market-neutral, and arbitrage, to gain exposure to cryptocurrencies and blockchain-based projects. Crypto hedge funds often provide institutional investors with more active management of their digital asset investments, using sophisticated trading strategies and risk management techniques. Many of these funds are managed by professionals with expertise in both traditional finance and cryptocurrencies, ensuring that institutional investors' capital is managed according to industry best practices. These funds may invest in a wide range of digital assets, from major cryptocurrencies like Bitcoin and Ethereum to emerging tokens in the DeFi and NFT spaces, offering a diversified approach to investing in the crypto market.

Digital Asset Custody Solutions are also integral to institutional investment vehicles. Institutional investors must ensure that their assets are stored securely, as they have regulatory obligations to protect client assets and mitigate the risk of theft or loss. Cryptocurrency custodians provide secure storage solutions for digital assets, employing advanced security measures such as multi-signature wallets, cold storage, and insurance to protect investor holdings. Major institutional custodians include companies like Coinbase Custody, BitGo, and Fidelity Digital Assets, which provide trusted custody services to institutional investors. These custodians ensure that cryptocurrencies are stored in a way that complies with regulations, offering peace of mind to institutional investors looking to enter the crypto market without exposing themselves to unnecessary risk.

Finally, **tokenized funds** are emerging as another vehicle for institutional investment in cryptocurrencies. These funds involve the tokenization of traditional assets or portfolios, allowing investors to buy shares in a portfolio of cryptocurrencies through blockchain-based tokens. Tokenized funds offer several advantages, including increased liquidity, fractional ownership, and greater transparency. By leveraging blockchain technology, tokenized funds can reduce the friction involved in asset management, providing institutional investors with a modern and efficient way to gain exposure to digital assets.

In conclusion, institutional investment vehicles have played a critical role in bridging the gap between traditional finance and the cryptocurrency market. These vehicles offer institutional investors a safe, efficient, and compliant way to gain exposure to digital assets, which has significantly contributed to the mainstream adoption of cryptocurrencies. As these investment vehicles continue to evolve and grow, they are expected to further institutionalize the cryptocurrency market, bringing more liquidity, stability, and regulatory clarity to the space. For institutional investors, these vehicles provide a pathway into the crypto market, while for the broader cryptocurrency ecosystem, they bring legitimacy and confidence, encouraging wider participation from all levels of the financial world.

The Ripple Effect on Market Dynamics

The involvement of institutional investors in the cryptocurrency market has created a ripple effect that is profoundly altering market dynamics. As more traditional financial institutions and large investors allocate capital into digital assets, the effects extend far beyond the immediate financial influx. Institutional participation influences liquidity, volatility, investor behavior, and even the development of new financial products. These shifts in market dynamics are reshaping the cryptocurrency landscape, making it more aligned with traditional financial markets while also introducing unique characteristics specific to digital assets. The ripple effect of institutional investment is not only driving significant changes in how cryptocurrencies are traded and valued but also in how they are perceived by both individual investors and regulatory bodies.

One of the most immediate impacts of institutional investment in cryptocurrencies is **increased liquidity**. Liquidity refers to the ease with which an asset can be bought or sold without causing a significant price change. Cryptocurrencies, particularly Bitcoin and Ethereum, have historically been plagued by liquidity constraints, often seeing price swings based on relatively low trading volumes. The influx of institutional capital brings substantial liquidity to the market, allowing larger transactions to be conducted without creating sharp price fluctuations. This increased liquidity benefits both retail and institutional investors by making the market more efficient and less prone to wild price swings, which have often been a concern for potential investors. With more liquid markets, it becomes easier for investors to enter and exit positions, encouraging broader participation and fostering more stability in the long term.

This increased liquidity also has an important effect on **market volatility**. While cryptocurrency markets are still more volatile than traditional asset classes, institutional involvement is beginning to reduce some of the erratic fluctuations that have characterized the sector. As institutional investors typically invest with a longer-term perspective, their capital flows are more stable and less prone to the speculative hype or panic that can drive short-term volatility in cryptocurrency markets. For example, the price of Bitcoin during the 2017 bull run saw massive fluctuations, driven largely by retail investors reacting to news and market sentiment. However, with institutional investors, who often take a more measured approach, the impact of irrational market behavior is somewhat mitigated. The result is a market that, over time, may experience less dramatic price swings, particularly during periods of heightened speculation or external market events.

The involvement of institutional investors is also influencing **market sentiment** in profound ways. In the early days of cryptocurrency, much of the sentiment was driven by the enthusiasm and fear of retail investors who were often drawn into the market by speculative hype. The narrative around Bitcoin and other digital assets was often framed in the media as a risky and untested venture, leading to wild price swings and market bubbles. With institutional players entering the space, the sentiment around cryptocurrencies has become more balanced. The capital and legitimacy that institutional investors bring to the market provide a sense of credibility, shifting the overall narrative from a speculative, fringe asset class to one that is seen as a more viable and established component of global finance. This shift in sentiment has a far-reaching impact, as it reassures retail investors and drives more confidence in the market, encouraging further participation.

Another significant ripple effect is the creation and development of **new financial products** aimed at institutional investors. As more institutional players look to gain exposure to cryptocurrencies, financial products like Bitcoin Futures, Exchange-Traded Funds (ETFs), and crypto-focused hedge funds are emerging to meet the demand. These products allow institutions to invest in digital assets while bypassing the complexities and risks associated with direct ownership of cryptocurrencies. Futures contracts, for instance, allow institutions to speculate on the price of Bitcoin without holding the asset itself, while ETFs provide a regulated way to gain exposure to Bitcoin and other cryptocurrencies. The introduction of these products opens up new avenues for institutional investors who may have been hesitant to directly engage with cryptocurrency exchanges due to concerns about custody, security, or regulatory uncertainty. The proliferation of such investment vehicles contributes to the continued mainstreaming of cryptocurrencies, offering greater accessibility and ease of entry for traditional investors.

Additionally, institutional involvement is driving the development of **custody solutions** and **regulatory frameworks** designed specifically for digital assets. In order to meet the needs of institutional investors, companies are developing secure and compliant custody solutions for holding cryptocurrencies. Institutional investors are required to follow strict regulations around asset custody, making secure storage of digital assets crucial. Leading custodians, such as Coinbase Custody and Fidelity Digital Assets, provide institutions with a way to store their digital assets securely, offering features like insurance coverage and multi-signature wallets to protect against theft or hacking. These advancements in custodial services, along with evolving regulatory frameworks, help build trust in the cryptocurrency ecosystem and make it more attractive to large investors. Regulatory clarity is also helping to shape market dynamics, as governments and regulators around the world begin to implement clearer guidelines for the buying, selling, and taxation of cryptocurrencies, further integrating them into the global financial system.

The ripple effect of institutional investment is also seen in the **increased development of blockchain technology**. As institutional investors seek to engage with the crypto market, they are also interested in the technological innovations that power these assets. This has led to greater investment in blockchain development, not only for cryptocurrencies but also for other use cases such as decentralized finance (DeFi), supply chain management, and smart contracts. The increased demand for blockchain technology from institutional investors accelerates innovation in the space, creating a feedback loop where institutional capital and technological advancement drive each other forward.

In conclusion, the ripple effect of institutional investment is reshaping the cryptocurrency market in ways that go beyond simply increasing capital flow. With greater liquidity, reduced volatility, and the development of new financial products, the entry of institutional investors is making cryptocurrencies more stable and integrated into the traditional financial system. Market sentiment has shifted, and as institutional investors continue to lead the charge, the future of cryptocurrencies looks increasingly promising as they move closer to full mainstream adoption. The ripple effect extends to the development of blockchain technology and the creation of secure, compliant infrastructure, all of which will play a vital role in the long-term success and maturation of the cryptocurrency market.

Chapter 5
Key Cryptocurrencies to Watch

As the cryptocurrency market continues to evolve, it's important for both new and seasoned investors to stay informed about the key digital assets that are driving the industry forward. While Bitcoin and Ethereum are the most recognized and widely adopted cryptocurrencies, there is a growing list of alternative coins, or altcoins, that are making waves in terms of technological innovation, real-world use cases, and investment potential. In this chapter, we will explore some of the most promising cryptocurrencies to watch in the coming years. Each of these digital assets has unique characteristics and plays a critical role in shaping the future of the cryptocurrency space.

Bitcoin, often referred to as "digital gold," remains the market leader and is a cornerstone of the entire cryptocurrency ecosystem. Its dominance in terms of market capitalization, adoption, and brand recognition makes it the most widely known and trusted cryptocurrency. However, as the industry matures, new contenders are emerging, bringing innovative features that aim to solve the limitations of Bitcoin and offer enhanced functionality. Ethereum, for example, has revolutionized the space by introducing smart contracts and enabling decentralized applications (DApps) through its blockchain. As more projects and developers build on top of Ethereum's network, its influence continues to grow, positioning it as one of the most critical assets in the blockchain ecosystem.

In addition to Bitcoin and Ethereum, other cryptocurrencies are gaining attention for their unique technological advances and utility in various sectors. From scalability improvements to privacy enhancements, these digital assets aim to address some of the biggest challenges faced by cryptocurrencies today. Projects like Solana, Polkadot, and Cardano, for instance, have gained significant traction due to their promise of faster, more efficient blockchains, which can handle larger volumes of transactions without sacrificing decentralization. Moreover, stablecoins, such as Tether and USD Coin, are becoming increasingly important for maintaining stability within the volatile crypto market, offering a bridge between traditional fiat currencies and digital assets. Understanding which cryptocurrencies are positioned for long-term success will help investors make informed decisions in a rapidly changing market.

Bitcoin: The Market Leader

Bitcoin, often referred to as the "king of cryptocurrency," remains the market leader in the digital asset space. Since its inception in 2009 by the anonymous entity Satoshi Nakamoto, Bitcoin has steadily cemented its place as the most recognized and widely adopted cryptocurrency, serving as a benchmark for the entire crypto market. As the first cryptocurrency to use blockchain technology, Bitcoin introduced a decentralized, peer-to-peer financial system that operates outside of traditional banking structures. Over a decade later, it continues to play a significant role in shaping the future of finance, making it a key asset to watch for both retail and institutional investors.

Bitcoin's dominance in the cryptocurrency market is evident through its market capitalization, which consistently accounts for a substantial portion of the total cryptocurrency market. It has set the standard for digital currencies and is often seen as a store of value, much like gold, which has led to its nickname "digital gold." This perception is primarily driven by Bitcoin's limited supply of 21 million coins, which makes it deflationary in nature. Unlike traditional fiat currencies, which can be printed at will by governments, Bitcoin's fixed supply ensures that it is resistant to inflationary pressures. This scarcity, coupled with growing demand, has helped Bitcoin gain credibility as a hedge against inflation, especially in times of economic uncertainty or when traditional financial systems experience instability.

Bitcoin's blockchain is a decentralized, immutable ledger that records all transactions without the need for intermediaries like banks. This decentralized nature allows Bitcoin to operate without the control of a central authority, offering users more autonomy and privacy compared to traditional financial systems. The underlying blockchain technology is secure, transparent, and transparent, making it difficult to alter or manipulate the transaction history. As the most well-established blockchain in the cryptocurrency space, Bitcoin's security features and decentralized governance model have set the foundation for subsequent digital assets to develop their own decentralized networks, contributing to the broader adoption of blockchain technology across industries.

While Bitcoin is often seen as a store of value, it is also used for various other purposes, such as a medium of exchange and a method for transferring money across borders. Bitcoin transactions are fast, cost-effective, and accessible to anyone with an internet connection, making it an attractive solution for individuals in countries with unstable financial systems or for those who need to send money internationally without the high fees associated with traditional remittance services. Bitcoin's use cases have expanded significantly, with businesses around the world accepting it as a form of payment for goods and services. High-profile companies like Tesla, Microsoft, and PayPal have embraced Bitcoin, integrating it into their business models and further validating its potential as a legitimate payment system.

The increasing institutional interest in Bitcoin has further solidified its position as the leader in the cryptocurrency market. Major investment firms, hedge funds, and even publicly traded companies have begun allocating Bitcoin to their portfolios, viewing it as a long-term investment asset. Bitcoin's ability to serve as a hedge against inflation and its growing acceptance by mainstream financial institutions have attracted large-scale investors, contributing to its overall value and liquidity. This institutional adoption has been instrumental in increasing Bitcoin's legitimacy and has helped bridge the gap between traditional finance and the emerging cryptocurrency market.

Despite its dominant position, Bitcoin is not without challenges. One of the primary concerns surrounding Bitcoin is its environmental impact. Bitcoin mining, the process by which new coins are created and transactions are verified, requires significant computational power and energy consumption. The environmental impact of Bitcoin mining has drawn criticism from environmentalists and governments alike, prompting some projects to explore alternative consensus mechanisms, such as proof of stake, which are more energy-efficient. However, many supporters of Bitcoin argue that the energy used for mining is necessary to maintain the security and integrity of the network, and that future innovations, such as the use of renewable energy sources for mining, will address these concerns.

Another challenge facing Bitcoin is scalability. The Bitcoin network can only handle a limited number of transactions per second, which has led to concerns about its ability to handle mass adoption and high transaction volumes. Solutions like the Lightning Network, a second-layer protocol that enables faster and cheaper transactions off-chain, are being developed to address these scalability issues. As the Bitcoin network evolves and solutions to these challenges are implemented, Bitcoin is expected to remain a key player in the cryptocurrency space, driving innovation and adoption.

In conclusion, Bitcoin continues to be the market leader in the cryptocurrency space due to its pioneering role in the development of blockchain technology, its decentralized nature, and its growing adoption as a store of value and medium of exchange. Bitcoin has overcome many obstacles over the years, including regulatory scrutiny and technological challenges, and its continued dominance is supported by its fixed supply, institutional adoption, and global recognition. As Bitcoin continues to mature and evolve, it will remain an essential asset for both investors and users, and its influence on the broader cryptocurrency ecosystem will only grow stronger. For anyone looking to understand the cryptocurrency market, Bitcoin remains the foundational asset to watch, as it continues to shape the future of digital finance.

Ethereum: Innovation Beyond Smart Contracts

Since its launch in 2015, Ethereum has emerged as the second most valuable cryptocurrency by market capitalization, surpassing many other digital assets in terms of technological innovation and adoption. Created by Vitalik Buterin and a team of developers, Ethereum was designed to address the limitations of Bitcoin, offering more than just a decentralized currency. Ethereum's introduction of

smart contracts revolutionized the blockchain space by enabling developers to build decentralized applications (DApps) on its platform. However, Ethereum's innovation goes far beyond smart contracts, and its influence extends across various industries, making it one of the most important assets in the cryptocurrency space.

At its core, Ethereum is a blockchain platform that facilitates the creation and execution of smart contracts. Smart contracts are self-executing contracts with the terms of the agreement directly written into code. They allow two parties to transact securely without the need for intermediaries, such as banks or lawyers. These contracts automatically execute when predefined conditions are met, ensuring trust and reducing the risk of fraud or human error. While Bitcoin's blockchain is primarily designed for financial transactions, Ethereum's blockchain supports a wide variety of use cases, making it the foundation for decentralized finance (DeFi), non-fungible tokens (NFTs), and decentralized autonomous organizations (DAOs).

Ethereum's ability to support decentralized applications (DApps) is one of its most important innovations. DApps are applications that run on a blockchain network, rather than on centralized servers, providing users with greater control over their data and reducing the risks of censorship and data manipulation. Ethereum's smart contracts enable DApps to operate autonomously, ensuring transparency and security. The Ethereum ecosystem has fostered a thriving developer community, and thousands of DApps have been built on the platform, ranging from financial services to gaming and social networking. The rise of DeFi platforms, for example, is largely attributable to Ethereum, which has allowed users to borrow, lend, trade, and earn interest on cryptocurrencies without the need for traditional financial intermediaries. Ethereum's support for DApps has fundamentally changed the way people think about applications and financial services, moving from centralized systems to decentralized alternatives.

Ethereum's influence extends beyond smart contracts and DApps to the realm of **non-fungible tokens (NFTs)**. NFTs are unique digital assets that represent ownership of specific items, such as digital art, collectibles, or virtual real estate. Ethereum's blockchain provides the infrastructure for NFTs through the ERC-721 token standard, which ensures the uniqueness and ownership of each token. NFTs gained mainstream attention in 2021 when high-profile art sales and celebrity endorsements pushed them into the public spotlight. Ethereum has become the primary platform for NFT transactions, and many artists and creators now use it to mint and sell their digital works. The explosion of the NFT market has solidified Ethereum's role as not only a digital currency platform but also a key player in the digital art and entertainment industries.

Ethereum's role in the blockchain space has also been bolstered by its focus on **scalability** and **sustainability**. While Ethereum's original proof-of-work (PoW) consensus mechanism shares similarities with Bitcoin's, it faced challenges in terms of scalability and high energy consumption. To address these issues, Ethereum is undergoing a significant upgrade called Ethereum 2.0, which aims to transition the network from PoW to **proof-of-stake (PoS)**. PoS is a more energy-efficient consensus mechanism that reduces the need for energy-intensive mining, allowing Ethereum to process more transactions per second and improve overall scalability. Ethereum 2.0 also introduces **sharding**, which divides the network into smaller, manageable pieces, enabling parallel processing and further increasing transaction throughput. This upgrade is expected to significantly enhance Ethereum's capacity to support the growing demand for decentralized applications, smart contracts, and other blockchain-based solutions.

Another key area of Ethereum's innovation is its growing **interoperability** with other blockchain networks. Interoperability refers to the ability for different blockchain networks to communicate and share information seamlessly. Ethereum has made strides in this area, with projects like **Polkadot** and **Cosmos** working to create a multichain ecosystem that allows different blockchains to operate together. Ethereum's developers are working on solutions to improve cross-chain communication, which will make it easier for users to move assets between different blockchain networks. This level of interoperability is essential for the future of the blockchain ecosystem, as it will help to create a more connected and collaborative environment for decentralized applications and services.

Ethereum's community-driven nature has also played a significant role in its success. The Ethereum network is open-source, meaning that anyone can contribute to its development. This has led to a highly active community of developers, researchers, and enthusiasts who are constantly working to improve the platform and push the boundaries of what is possible with blockchain technology. Ethereum's decentralized governance model allows the community to propose and vote on changes to the network, ensuring that the platform evolves in a way that meets the needs of its users.

In conclusion, Ethereum's innovation extends far beyond its role as the first platform to introduce smart contracts. Its impact on decentralized finance, non-fungible tokens, and blockchain scalability has made it one of the most important and influential assets in the cryptocurrency space. Ethereum's ability to support decentralized applications, coupled with its focus on sustainability and interoperability, positions it as a foundational layer of the decentralized web. With Ethereum 2.0 and other ongoing upgrades, the platform is well-poised to continue driving innovation and adoption in the blockchain space, cementing its position as a key player in the future of digital finance and decentralized technologies.

Emerging Altcoins with High Potential

The cryptocurrency market is often dominated by Bitcoin and Ethereum, but emerging altcoins are gaining traction for their unique features, technological innovations, and growing adoption. These altcoins, which are alternatives to Bitcoin, represent a diverse range of blockchain projects that are addressing different problems and offering solutions that could transform industries like finance, supply chain management, healthcare, and more. With their potential to disrupt existing markets and innovate beyond what Bitcoin and Ethereum have achieved, these emerging altcoins are attracting investors and developers alike. Below are a few of the most promising emerging altcoins that have the potential to make significant impacts in the near future.

One such emerging altcoin is **Solana (SOL)**. Solana is a high-performance blockchain designed to provide scalable, fast, and low-cost transactions. Unlike Ethereum, which often suffers from high gas fees and congestion due to its proof-of-work consensus mechanism, Solana uses a unique consensus called **proof-of-history (PoH)** combined with proof-of-stake (PoS). This allows it to process transactions quickly—up to 65,000 transactions per second—without sacrificing decentralization. Solana's speed and low transaction costs make it an attractive platform for decentralized applications (DApps) and decentralized finance (DeFi) projects. It has gained significant attention from developers and investors, with numerous DeFi platforms, NFTs, and DApps being built on its network. The growing ecosystem surrounding Solana makes it a strong contender for Ethereum's dominance in the smart contract platform space.

Another altcoin worth mentioning is **Cardano (ADA)**. Cardano is a blockchain platform built on the proof-of-stake consensus mechanism, focusing on security, scalability, and sustainability. Cardano's approach differs from Ethereum's by focusing on peer-reviewed research and academic rigor in its development. It uses the **Ouroboros PoS protocol**, which is designed to be energy-efficient while providing security and decentralization. Cardano has been building its ecosystem slowly but steadily, with significant upgrades like **smart contract functionality** introduced through the Alonzo hard fork. With an emphasis on improving real-world applications, Cardano is particularly focused on empowering developing countries by providing secure and low-cost financial solutions. Its ability to attract partnerships, especially in Africa, where it aims to provide blockchain solutions to improve education, agriculture, and finance, positions Cardano as an altcoin with substantial long-term potential.

Polkadot (DOT) is another exciting emerging altcoin that is designed to solve the issue of blockchain interoperability. While many blockchain platforms operate in isolation, Polkadot enables different blockchains to communicate and share information seamlessly through its **parachain** model. This allows for greater scalability and enables decentralized applications to access multiple blockchains simultaneously. Polkadot's interoperability feature is crucial as it creates a multi-chain ecosystem, improving the efficiency of blockchain networks. Its underlying technology has attracted many developers, and the Polkadot network has seen growing interest, particularly for projects that need to interact across multiple blockchains. As interoperability becomes a more significant focus in the cryptocurrency space, Polkadot's unique position in this area could propel it to new heights.

Avalanche (AVAX) is another altcoin with considerable potential due to its focus on scalability and transaction speed. Avalanche is a smart contract platform that aims to solve the scalability issues faced by Ethereum by offering near-instant finality and extremely low transaction costs. The network claims to be capable of processing up to 4,500 transactions per second, making it one of the fastest blockchains in the market. Avalanche uses a consensus mechanism called **Avalanche Consensus**, which combines elements of proof-of-stake and a novel approach to ensuring consensus across multiple validators. With a growing ecosystem of decentralized finance projects, NFTs, and enterprise-level applications, Avalanche is positioning itself as a key player in the next generation of blockchain technology.

Terra (LUNA) is another altcoin gaining significant attention in the DeFi and stablecoin ecosystem. Terra's primary innovation lies in its ability to create **algorithmic stablecoins** that are backed by its native token, LUNA. The most well-known of these is **UST**, a stablecoin pegged to the US dollar. Terra's blockchain supports a wide range of financial applications, including lending, borrowing, and payments, and its stablecoins are used within the platform to facilitate transactions and provide liquidity. The Terra ecosystem has seen rapid growth, particularly in decentralized finance (DeFi), and its ability to offer a decentralized stablecoin solution has drawn significant interest. With the broader DeFi market continuing to grow, Terra's approach to decentralized and algorithmically backed stablecoins could help it gain a larger share of the market.

Finally, **Chainlink (LINK)** is an altcoin that facilitates decentralized oracles—systems that bring off-chain data to on-chain smart contracts. Chainlink's technology allows smart contracts to access real-world information, such as prices, weather data, and other external inputs, which is crucial for many decentralized applications, particularly in the DeFi sector. Chainlink has become an integral part of the DeFi ecosystem by enabling more advanced and automated financial services. Its importance in bridging the gap between real-world data and blockchain applications has made it a highly valuable project with significant growth potential.

In conclusion, the cryptocurrency market is filled with emerging altcoins that offer unique solutions and have the potential to challenge or complement Bitcoin and Ethereum. Projects like Solana, Cardano, Polkadot, Avalanche, Terra, and Chainlink are just a few examples of how innovation in blockchain technology is rapidly expanding the possibilities for decentralized applications, finance, and interoperability. Each of these altcoins addresses key issues like scalability, transaction speed, and blockchain compatibility, which are essential for the widespread adoption of cryptocurrencies. As these projects continue to evolve and gain traction, they could play a significant role in shaping the future of blockchain technology and cryptocurrency. For investors looking to diversify their portfolios or gain exposure to new and promising blockchain projects, these emerging altcoins offer high potential opportunities.

Chapter 6
The Bull Run Begins: Timing and Entry Points

As the cryptocurrency market experiences periods of exponential growth, the onset of a bull run presents significant opportunities for investors. A bull run, marked by rising prices and increasing market optimism, can be both thrilling and overwhelming. While these periods of growth are often seen as a time to make substantial profits, the key to success during a bull run lies in recognizing the right moment to enter the market. The timing of entry plays a critical role in maximizing returns and minimizing the risks of buying in at inflated prices. In this chapter, we will explore how to identify the beginning of a bull run, assess market conditions, and determine optimal entry points for both short-term traders and long-term investors.

Identifying the early signs of a bull run is essential for any investor looking to capitalize on the growth potential of cryptocurrencies. While markets are often unpredictable, there are specific indicators and patterns that can signal the start of a bull run. These include technical signals like breakouts above key resistance levels, increases in trading volume, and the general shift in market sentiment from fear to optimism. Understanding these early indicators can provide investors with an edge, allowing them to position themselves before the bulk of the market catches on. By recognizing the signals that typically precede a bull run, investors can make informed decisions about when to enter the market and avoid the common mistake of buying in too late.

Once the signs of a bull run are identified, determining the best entry points becomes the next critical step. Buying during the initial phase of a bull run offers the highest potential for gains, but it also requires a keen understanding of market cycles and technical analysis. Entry points can vary depending on an investor's strategy — whether it's to take advantage of short-term price movements or to position for long-term growth. Strategies such as dollar-cost averaging (DCA), which involves buying at regular intervals regardless of price fluctuations, can help investors mitigate risks and ensure they are buying at favorable times. In this chapter, we will discuss various techniques and strategies for determining the right time to enter a bull market, providing readers with the tools they need to make smarter investment decisions.

Spotting Early Indicators of a Bull Market

Spotting the early signs of a bull market is crucial for investors who want to capitalize on upward price trends before they become fully realized. A bull market, characterized by sustained increases in asset prices, can present significant opportunities for wealth accumulation, but it requires timely entry to maximize returns. The challenge lies in identifying these early indicators, which often emerge long before mainstream media and the general public catch on. By recognizing the signs of a bull market early, investors can position themselves advantageously, increasing the likelihood of substantial profits while mitigating the risk of entering the market too late.

One of the most common early indicators of a bull market is a **shift in market sentiment**. Cryptocurrency markets, like other financial markets, are heavily influenced by investor psychology. During periods of uncertainty or stagnation, market sentiment tends to be bearish, with pessimism dominating. However, a shift in sentiment can signal the start of a bull run. When market sentiment transitions from fear and uncertainty to optimism and confidence, the first signs of a potential bull market emerge. This shift is often accompanied by an increase in social media discussions, positive news stories, and increasing interest from new investors. A significant factor that drives this shift is the entry of institutional investors, who bring liquidity and credibility to the market, sparking further enthusiasm. Watching sentiment indicators—such as social media activity, community discussions, and mainstream news coverage—can provide valuable insight into when optimism is beginning to take hold, signaling the early stages of a bull market.

Another key indicator to watch for is **technical analysis signals**, particularly in the form of breakouts above key resistance levels. Resistance levels are price points where an asset has historically faced selling pressure, preventing it from rising further. When the price of an asset breaks through these resistance levels, it often signals that buying pressure is overwhelming the market, creating a strong upward trend. For example, Bitcoin or Ethereum might have previously faced resistance around a specific price point, but once the price pushes above this level, it can indicate that a new bull market is forming. Traders often use chart patterns, such as **ascending triangles** or **cup and handle formations**, to anticipate breakouts. In addition, volume plays a crucial role in confirming the validity of a breakout. A breakout accompanied by higher-than-usual trading volume indicates that the move is backed by strong market participation, further validating the likelihood of a bull market.

The **moving average crossover** is another valuable technical indicator to spot the beginning of a bull market. Moving averages smooth out price data to help identify trends over time. A commonly used strategy is to observe the crossover of a shorter-term moving average (such as the 50-day moving average) above a longer-term moving average (such as the 200-day moving average). This is known as a "Golden Cross," a bullish signal that indicates upward momentum. When the short-term moving average crosses above the long-term moving average, it suggests that recent price action is turning more bullish, signaling the beginning of a potential bull market. Traders and investors often use this crossover as a signal to enter the market, as it suggests that momentum is shifting in favor of the bulls. It is important to note that this indicator should be used in conjunction with other analysis tools to confirm the market's direction.

Another critical sign of a bull market is the **increase in trading volume**. Volume measures the number of assets being traded within a given period and is a critical component in assessing the strength of a price move. A significant increase in volume during a price rise indicates that the market is strongly supporting the upward movement. Volume spikes often accompany breakout patterns, confirming that the buying activity is robust and that the price trend is likely to continue. Conversely, low volume during a price increase could indicate weak market support and a higher risk of a price reversal. During the early stages of a bull market, volume typically increases gradually, reflecting growing interest and participation from both retail and institutional investors. Traders often use volume as a key confirmation tool, especially when paired with other technical indicators, to ensure that the price move is not a temporary anomaly.

Finally, **macroeconomic factors** and **external market catalysts** can also serve as early indicators of a bull market. In the cryptocurrency space, the introduction of favorable regulations, technological advancements, and institutional adoption can trigger widespread enthusiasm, setting the stage for a bull market. For example, news of a country's acceptance of Bitcoin as legal tender, like El Salvador's adoption in 2021, can spark a surge in buying activity, signaling the beginning of a bull run. Similarly, the approval of cryptocurrency ETFs or other financial products by regulatory bodies like the U.S. Securities and Exchange Commission (SEC) can instill confidence in the market, attracting institutional capital and fueling price growth. These external factors often provide the catalyst that ignites the broader market, and their influence should not be overlooked when evaluating the early signs of a bull market.

In conclusion, spotting the early indicators of a bull market involves a combination of technical analysis, market sentiment, volume trends, and macroeconomic factors. By watching for a shift in sentiment from fear to optimism, identifying breakouts above resistance levels, observing moving average crossovers, and monitoring increased trading volume, investors can position themselves to capitalize on the early stages of a bull run. Additionally, being aware of external factors, such as regulatory changes and technological advancements, can provide valuable context for understanding the broader market dynamics. Recognizing these early indicators can give investors a significant advantage, helping them enter the market at the right time and potentially enjoy substantial returns during a bull market.

Analyzing Buy Signals

In cryptocurrency trading, analyzing buy signals is an essential part of developing a successful investment strategy. A buy signal is an indicator or set of indicators that suggests it might be an opportune time to purchase an asset, based on specific market conditions, technical analysis, or sentiment shifts. Understanding how to interpret these signals accurately can help investors and traders maximize their chances of making profitable trades, while minimizing risks. Buy signals can come from various sources, including price action, chart patterns, technical indicators, and fundamental analysis. By using a combination of these tools, investors can make more informed decisions and optimize their entry points into the market.

One of the most widely used methods for identifying buy signals is **technical analysis**. Technical analysis relies on historical price data and volume to forecast future price movements. One of the most basic yet effective buy signals comes from **support levels**. Support refers to a price point at which an asset's price tends to find buying interest and stops falling. When a cryptocurrency's price drops to a key support level and holds steady, it often signals that the market has found a floor, and buying pressure may be starting to push the price higher. Traders often use support levels as buy signals, particularly when they appear to be respected after a short-term decline. If the price starts to bounce back from this support level, it indicates that the market is likely to trend upwards, providing a solid entry point for potential buyers.

Another important technical tool to analyze buy signals is the **Moving Average Convergence Divergence (MACD)** indicator. The MACD is a momentum oscillator that tracks the difference between two moving averages, usually the 12-day and 26-day exponential moving averages (EMA). A common buy signal occurs when the MACD line crosses above the signal line, particularly when the asset has been in a period of downward or sideways movement. This crossover indicates that the momentum is shifting to the upside, and the market is potentially entering a new bullish phase. Additionally, traders often look for MACD divergence—when the price of an asset forms lower lows, but the MACD forms higher lows, indicating that the downtrend may be weakening and a reversal could be imminent.

Relative Strength Index (RSI) is another widely used indicator for analyzing buy signals. RSI is a momentum oscillator that measures the speed and change of price movements, providing insight into whether an asset is overbought or oversold. RSI values range from 0 to 100, with readings below 30 generally indicating that an asset is oversold (a potential buy signal) and readings above 70 signaling that the asset may be overbought. When the RSI dips below 30 and then rises above it, this can be considered a bullish reversal signal. It suggests that selling pressure is diminishing, and buying pressure is starting to take control. The RSI can be particularly useful in identifying buy signals during periods of market correction or consolidation, where an asset is poised for a rebound.

Another common buy signal comes from the **Golden Cross**, which occurs when a short-term moving average, such as the 50-day moving average, crosses above a long-term moving average, such as the 200-day moving average. This technical pattern is seen as a strong bullish signal, as it indicates that the recent price action is trending upward and could continue to rise. The Golden Cross is often followed by a period of strong price appreciation, making it an important buy signal for traders looking to capitalize on an emerging bull trend. The reverse of the Golden Cross, the **Death Cross**, occurs when the short-term moving average crosses below the long-term moving average, signaling a bearish trend, so its absence during the Golden Cross gives greater confidence to the buy signal.

Chart patterns can also provide critical buy signals. One of the most well-known patterns is the **cup and handle formation**. This pattern resembles the shape of a tea cup and indicates a period of consolidation before a breakout. The "cup" forms as the price declines and then begins to rise, while the "handle" appears as a brief consolidation or pullback before the price breaks out upwards. The breakout, often coupled with increasing volume, serves as a confirmation of the buy signal, suggesting that the price is poised to continue its upward movement. Traders often wait for the price to break above the resistance line formed at the lip of the cup before executing a buy order.

While technical indicators and chart patterns are incredibly useful for identifying buy signals, **fundamental analysis** also plays an important role in analyzing market conditions. For example, a positive announcement such as a cryptocurrency project's upgrade or partnership, new regulations, or institutional investment can trigger a buy signal. Fundamental analysis involves looking at the broader picture—whether the project's fundamentals are strong and whether there are underlying factors that could drive demand for the cryptocurrency in the future. In the case of Bitcoin, for instance, buy signals might be triggered by developments related to institutional adoption, network upgrades, or macroeconomic events like inflationary concerns that increase demand for digital assets as a hedge against fiat currency devaluation.

Sentiment analysis, which gauges the mood of the market, is also a useful tool for identifying buy signals. In the crypto space, sentiment can be heavily influenced by social media, news coverage, and the opinions of influential figures. When there is a marked shift in sentiment from fear to optimism, it often signals the early stages of a bull run, providing an entry point for investors. Tools that track social media mentions, news sentiment, and community engagement can offer valuable insights into when a positive sentiment shift is occurring, and when it might be time to buy.

In conclusion, analyzing buy signals involves a combination of technical indicators, chart patterns, fundamental analysis, and sentiment tracking. Identifying key support levels, MACD crossovers, RSI reversals, Golden Cross patterns, and emerging trends in the broader market can all provide valuable insights into when to enter the market. A careful analysis of these signals, combined with a disciplined approach to risk management, can help investors make informed decisions that maximize their chances of success in the cryptocurrency market. By learning to spot these buy signals early, traders and investors can position themselves to take advantage of emerging trends and ride the wave of a bull market.

Making Your First Investment During the Run

Making your first investment during a cryptocurrency bull run can be an exciting and potentially lucrative experience. However, it's essential to approach this phase of investing with a clear strategy and an understanding of the risks involved. Bull runs are marked by rising prices and increasing optimism, which can create a sense of urgency for investors to jump in before prices climb higher. While the potential for high returns is appealing, entering the market without proper planning can lead to significant losses, particularly if the market experiences volatility or reversals. This guide will walk you through the steps of making your first investment during a bull run, emphasizing the importance of strategy, timing, and risk management.

Before making any investment, it's crucial to do thorough **research**. Understand the cryptocurrency you plan to invest in, its use case, market dynamics, and potential for long-term growth. The first step should involve identifying a strong, well-established cryptocurrency, such as Bitcoin or Ethereum, or exploring promising altcoins with solid technological fundamentals. Research the project's whitepaper, team, and community support, as well as market sentiment. Bull runs tend to bring a wave of new investors, and not all cryptocurrencies are equally equipped to maintain growth. Investing in well-established, reputable assets is generally a safer approach than chasing newer, untested projects during periods of high hype. Ensure you are investing in an asset you believe in, and avoid making decisions based solely on price speculation.

Once you've chosen a cryptocurrency, **determine your investment amount**. It's tempting during a bull run to invest a large portion of your capital, driven by the fear of missing out (FOMO), but this can be risky. It's essential to start with an amount that you can afford to lose, as markets can experience sudden corrections. Many experienced investors recommend the strategy of **dollar-cost averaging (DCA)**, which involves investing a fixed amount of money at regular intervals, regardless of the asset's price. DCA reduces the risk of investing all your capital at the peak of a market rally and helps you avoid buying in when prices are overly inflated. Instead of trying to time the market perfectly, DCA allows you to spread your risk over time and build your position gradually as the market fluctuates.

When entering the market during a bull run, **timing your entry point** is critical. The earlier you can identify the start of a bull run, the better your chances of making a profitable investment. However, the challenge is that bull markets often come with high volatility, and it's difficult to predict when the best entry point will occur. One way to time your entry is to look for **support levels** and **breakouts** in price action. When the price of an asset repeatedly bounces off a specific support level, it suggests that buying interest is strong and the asset may be preparing for upward movement. A breakout above previous resistance levels, coupled with increased trading volume, can also be a signal that the bull run is gaining momentum. Technical indicators like the **MACD crossover** or **Relative Strength Index (RSI)** can further help confirm your decision to enter. The key is not to rush in at the first sign of price increases but to wait for a confirmation of strong bullish momentum.

Another important aspect of investing during a bull run is **managing your risk**. While bull markets can offer significant returns, they also carry the risk of a sharp reversal. It's vital to have a plan in place to protect your capital if the market takes a downturn. One effective way to manage risk is to set **stop-loss orders**, which automatically sell your position if the price drops to a certain threshold. For example, if you purchase a cryptocurrency at $50,000 and set a stop-loss at 10% below that price, the order will trigger a sale if the price falls to $45,000. This allows you to limit losses and protect your investment in case of sudden market corrections. Additionally, consider setting **take-profit levels** at certain price targets, allowing you to lock in profits when the price reaches a point you're comfortable with.

It's also wise to diversify your investments during a bull run, especially if you're new to cryptocurrency. Instead of putting all your funds into one asset, consider spreading your investment across several cryptocurrencies, including both established coins and emerging altcoins. Diversification helps reduce risk, as the performance of different assets may vary during the bull run. While Bitcoin and Ethereum are the most well-known cryptocurrencies, many altcoins offer unique features or solve different problems, potentially yielding higher returns. However, be cautious with smaller, lesser-known coins, as they can be highly speculative and subject to extreme volatility.

Lastly, **stay disciplined and avoid emotional decisions**. Bull runs can create a sense of urgency, leading some investors to make impulsive decisions driven by excitement or fear. FOMO can cause people to buy at inflated prices, only to see their investments lose value when the market corrects. It's important to stick to your plan, resist the urge to chase prices, and remember that the market can fluctuate rapidly. Even if you miss an early entry point, patience and strategic investing will often yield better results in the long run.

In conclusion, making your first investment during a cryptocurrency bull run requires careful planning, research, and risk management. By selecting the right cryptocurrency, investing gradually through dollar-cost averaging, and waiting for favorable entry points, you can maximize your chances of success. Implementing protective measures like stop-loss orders, diversifying your portfolio, and staying disciplined will help you navigate the volatility of a bull market and avoid costly mistakes. Bull runs offer incredible opportunities for growth, but they also come with inherent risks—by preparing thoroughly and investing wisely, you can make the most of these opportunities while protecting your investment.

Chapter 7
Navigating Volatility

Cryptocurrency markets are notorious for their volatility, which can present both significant opportunities and risks for investors. Unlike traditional financial markets, which tend to experience more gradual price movements, the crypto market is highly susceptible to sudden and extreme fluctuations. These price swings can be caused by various factors, including market sentiment, news events, regulatory changes, technological developments, and large institutional transactions. While volatility creates the potential for high returns, it also increases the risk of substantial losses. In this chapter, we will explore how to effectively navigate the volatility of the cryptocurrency market, providing strategies for managing risk and making informed decisions during periods of rapid price movements.

Understanding the nature of volatility is essential for any investor in the crypto space. Volatility is often driven by the emotions of market participants, with fear and greed playing pivotal roles in price fluctuations. When prices rise rapidly, the market can become driven by FOMO (fear of missing out), encouraging even more buying, which pushes prices higher. Conversely, negative news, regulatory concerns, or a shift in sentiment can trigger mass selling, leading to sharp declines. Recognizing the psychological aspects of market movements and the triggers behind volatility can help investors make more rational decisions and avoid emotional reactions to sudden price changes.

Successfully navigating volatility requires the use of effective risk management strategies. While it's tempting to ride the waves of price swings, it's crucial to protect your capital and avoid making impulsive decisions. Tools such as stop-loss orders, portfolio diversification, and setting clear entry and exit points can help investors stay grounded during volatile periods. By understanding the risks and implementing strategies that balance potential rewards with risk, investors can better position themselves to profit during bullish phases and minimize losses during downturns. This chapter will provide you with the tools and mindset needed to handle cryptocurrency volatility effectively, turning potential challenges into opportunities for growth.

Understanding Market Fluctuations

Understanding market fluctuations is critical for anyone participating in the cryptocurrency market. The high volatility of digital assets, which often experience rapid and dramatic price movements, is one of the defining characteristics of this market. These fluctuations, while presenting opportunities for significant profits, also come with risks. To navigate the crypto space effectively, it's important to understand the factors that drive market fluctuations and how they influence price movements. By identifying the underlying causes of market fluctuations, investors can make more informed decisions, manage risks, and potentially capitalize on price movements in the volatile cryptocurrency market.

One of the primary drivers of market fluctuations is **market sentiment**. Sentiment refers to the overall mood or attitude of investors toward an asset or the market as a whole. Cryptocurrency markets are particularly sensitive to sentiment, as emotions like fear, greed, and excitement can cause sharp price movements in a short period. When sentiment is positive, often due to news about a major technological development, institutional adoption, or positive regulatory announcements, it can lead to rapid price increases. Conversely, negative sentiment, triggered by factors such as regulatory crackdowns, security breaches, or unfavorable news, can lead to mass sell-offs and a decline in prices. Understanding the psychology of the market is essential, as sentiment-driven price movements often precede fundamental changes and can provide valuable trading signals.

Another factor contributing to market fluctuations is **news and external events**. The cryptocurrency market is highly reactive to news and developments, especially when it comes to regulatory changes, technological advancements, and macroeconomic factors. For example, when a government announces favorable regulations or recognizes cryptocurrency as a legal tender, it can lead to a surge in buying activity, causing prices to rise. Similarly, unfavorable news, such as regulatory crackdowns or security issues affecting large cryptocurrency exchanges, can lead to panic selling and a decrease in asset prices. These news-driven fluctuations can be particularly volatile, as the market often reacts quickly to headlines, even when the underlying facts may not fully reflect the long-term implications. Investors who stay informed and understand the potential impact of these external events can better anticipate and react to market fluctuations.

Market manipulation is another factor that can contribute to price fluctuations, especially in the relatively nascent cryptocurrency market. Due to the decentralized and often unregulated nature of crypto exchanges, markets can be more susceptible to manipulation than traditional financial markets. Large players, including institutional investors or "whales" (individuals or entities that control large amounts of a cryptocurrency), can significantly influence prices by executing large buy or sell orders. This type of manipulation can create artificial price movements, leading to short-term fluctuations that may not reflect the true value of an asset. One common tactic is "pump and dump" schemes, where the price of a cryptocurrency is artificially inflated by coordinated buying, only for the manipulators to sell off their holdings at the peak, leaving other investors with significant losses. Understanding the risks of market manipulation and using tools like technical analysis can help investors avoid falling victim to these price swings.

Supply and demand is another fundamental factor that drives market fluctuations. Cryptocurrencies are often designed with a fixed or limited supply, creating an inherent scarcity that can influence demand. Bitcoin, for example, has a maximum supply of 21 million coins, which makes it susceptible to price fluctuations based on shifts in demand. When demand increases, whether due to institutional adoption, growing use cases, or positive market sentiment, the price tends to rise. Conversely, when demand decreases, perhaps due to a market correction or loss of confidence in the asset, prices can fall. In addition, factors such as the **halving event** in Bitcoin, which reduces the rate at which new coins are mined, can have significant implications for supply and, by extension, price. Events that impact the supply and demand balance, such as changes in the mining reward structure or an increase in adoption, can lead to substantial price fluctuations.

The **liquidity** of a cryptocurrency also plays a role in its price volatility. Liquidity refers to how easily an asset can be bought or sold without causing significant price changes. Cryptocurrencies with lower liquidity are more susceptible to large price swings because it takes fewer transactions to move the market. In contrast, assets with higher liquidity, like Bitcoin and Ethereum, are less prone to sudden price movements because there is a larger pool of buyers and sellers. Market fluctuations are more exaggerated in smaller, less liquid cryptocurrencies, where a single large buy or sell order can significantly impact the price. As more investors and institutions enter the market, liquidity improves, which can help reduce volatility and create a more stable market environment.

In addition to external factors, **technical analysis** plays a crucial role in understanding market fluctuations. Technical analysis involves studying historical price data and using various indicators, such as moving averages, Relative Strength Index (RSI), and Bollinger Bands, to predict future price movements. By analyzing price patterns and trends, traders can identify key support and resistance levels, overbought or oversold conditions, and potential price breakouts or reversals. Technical analysis provides a more structured approach to understanding market fluctuations, allowing investors to make informed decisions based on historical data and current market conditions rather than relying solely on emotional reactions to price changes.

In conclusion, understanding market fluctuations in the cryptocurrency space requires a multi-faceted approach that takes into account market sentiment, news events, supply and demand dynamics, liquidity, and technical analysis. Cryptocurrency markets are highly reactive and prone to significant price swings due to the emotional nature of market participants, external factors like regulatory changes, and the unique characteristics of digital assets. By staying informed, managing risk, and using technical tools, investors can navigate market fluctuations more effectively and position themselves for success in a volatile environment. Recognizing the drivers behind market fluctuations and adapting to them with sound strategies is essential for achieving long-term profitability in the cryptocurrency market.

The Psychology of Crypto Trading

The psychology of crypto trading plays a significant role in determining the success or failure of an investor's decisions in the cryptocurrency market. Cryptocurrencies, known for their high volatility and rapid price movements, often trigger intense emotions, which can cloud judgment and lead to impulsive, reactive behavior. Understanding the psychological factors at play in crypto trading is essential for maintaining discipline, managing risk, and making sound investment decisions. In this highly speculative market, the emotional responses of traders—such as fear, greed, and overconfidence—can heavily influence the market's behavior and the outcomes for individual investors.

Fear and Greed: The Two Primary Drivers

Fear and greed are the primary emotional drivers in the cryptocurrency market, and they often lead to significant price swings. Fear is particularly prominent during market downturns or when prices experience sudden drops. It can cause traders to panic and sell off their positions in a hurry, leading to further price declines. The fear of missing out (FOMO) is also a powerful force during bull runs, where investors, driven by the fear of losing out on potential gains, rush into the market without fully understanding the risks. This can cause unsustainable price increases, creating asset bubbles that may eventually burst when reality sets in.

Greed, on the other hand, often emerges during bullish trends, when traders experience euphoric rallies and start to believe that prices will keep rising indefinitely. This greed-driven mentality can lead investors to take on more risk than they should, pushing them to over-leverage their positions or enter the market at inflated prices. The desire to maximize profits can cloud judgment, resulting in the purchase of assets at unsustainable levels. Both fear and greed can result in a cycle of buying high and selling low—one of the most common mistakes traders make, especially in volatile markets like cryptocurrency.

Overconfidence and Overtrading

Overconfidence is another psychological pitfall in crypto trading. After a series of profitable trades, traders may develop an inflated sense of their abilities, leading them to take on excessive risk. Overconfident traders might assume they can predict market movements with certainty, even though cryptocurrency markets are unpredictable by nature. This often leads to poor decision-making, such as taking larger positions than originally planned, or ignoring proper risk management techniques like stop-loss orders.

Overconfidence can also result in **overtrading**, which occurs when traders make excessive trades based on their belief that they can time the market perfectly. The desire to be constantly involved in market action, even during neutral or sideways market conditions, can result in taking unnecessary risks and eroding profits with repeated small losses. Overtrading often stems from impatience or the belief that one can always profit by making frequent trades, but in reality, this approach increases transaction costs and the risk of losses, especially in highly volatile markets.

Loss Aversion and Confirmation Bias

Loss aversion is a psychological phenomenon in which traders experience the pain of losses more intensely than the pleasure of gains. This often leads investors to hold onto losing positions for too long, hoping that the price will eventually recover. Rather than cutting their losses and moving on, traders often refuse to sell at a loss, convinced that they can recover the lost value. This behavior can lead to significant losses, as the market may continue to trend downward, further deepening the losses. The desire to avoid realizing losses can prevent traders from making rational decisions and sticking to their original strategies.

Confirmation bias is another common cognitive bias that can cloud a trader's judgment. Traders often seek out information that confirms their existing beliefs or opinions about the market, while ignoring contradictory data. In crypto trading, this bias can manifest when traders focus on positive news or bullish predictions while disregarding negative developments or bearish trends. This selective perception leads to poor decision-making and can result in holding onto positions that are not supported by the market's broader fundamentals. By failing to assess all available information objectively, traders may miss out on early warning signs of a market correction or reversal.

The Role of FOMO (Fear of Missing Out)

The fear of missing out (FOMO) is a powerful psychological force in cryptocurrency markets, where sudden price movements can lead to swift, emotional decisions. FOMO occurs when traders see others profiting from an asset's rise and feel the need to act quickly to capture the same opportunity. This fear often leads to buying into a market after prices have already surged, driven by the irrational belief that the upward movement will continue indefinitely. Unfortunately, the market may be at or near its peak, and by entering late, FOMO-driven traders often find themselves facing steep losses when the market corrects. FOMO is particularly prevalent during bull runs, where media hype and social media discussions can amplify the sense of urgency to join the market.

Managing the Psychology of Crypto Trading

To succeed in the volatile world of crypto trading, it is crucial to manage emotions and maintain discipline. One of the most effective ways to mitigate emotional decision-making is by creating and sticking to a **trading plan**. A well-defined plan includes clear entry and exit points, as well as stop-loss orders to minimize risk. By setting limits on how much to invest, how much risk is acceptable, and when to sell, traders can avoid acting on impulse and make more rational decisions. Additionally, it's important to **diversify** investments and not put all capital into a single asset, thereby reducing the impact of market fluctuations on the overall portfolio.

Another key strategy is to avoid looking at the market constantly. Monitoring the market too frequently can fuel emotional reactions to short-term price fluctuations, increasing anxiety and making it harder to maintain a long-term perspective. Regularly taking a step back to assess the overall market situation and adjust strategies accordingly is crucial for maintaining a rational mindset.

Finally, **mindfulness and emotional control** are vital components of successful trading. Recognizing the emotions at play—whether it's fear, greed, overconfidence, or FOMO—can help traders manage their psychological responses and avoid making decisions based on impulse. Developing self-discipline and emotional resilience can be the difference between success and failure in the unpredictable world of cryptocurrency trading.

In conclusion, understanding and managing the psychology of crypto trading is key to long-term success. By recognizing emotional drivers like fear, greed, and FOMO, traders can make more informed, rational decisions, avoid common pitfalls, and stick to their strategies. Maintaining discipline and emotional control, combined with a well-thought-out trading plan, helps investors navigate the complexities of the crypto market with greater confidence and less risk.

Staying Calm During Market Corrections

Market corrections are a natural and inevitable part of any financial market, including cryptocurrencies, which are known for their volatility. A correction refers to a short-term decline in asset prices—typically a drop of 10% or more from recent highs. While corrections can be unsettling, they present opportunities for astute investors who are prepared to handle them with calm and rationality. Understanding the nature of market corrections and employing strategies to stay composed during these downturns is key to managing risk and protecting investments in a volatile market. In this article, we will explore how to stay calm during market corrections, focusing on mindset, strategies, and best practices for making informed decisions when the market experiences a dip.

First and foremost, it is essential to recognize that **market corrections are a normal part of market cycles**. They often occur after a period of strong price growth, where investors start to take profits and some level of market fatigue sets in. Corrections provide the market with an opportunity to reset, allowing for healthy price consolidation before the next potential upward trend. Understanding this cyclical nature can help investors avoid panicking when prices fall. Rather than viewing a market correction as a sign of disaster, investors should reframe it as a healthy correction—a normal event that cleanses the market and allows for stronger, more sustainable growth in the future. This mindset shift helps prevent emotional decision-making and positions investors for long-term success.

Avoiding emotional reactions during a market correction is one of the most important factors in maintaining composure. Fear is a natural response to losing money, but allowing fear to drive decisions during a correction can lead to poor outcomes, such as selling assets at a loss in a panic. Fear of missing out (FOMO) or fear of further losses can make investors act impulsively, locking in losses that may have been avoided if they had stayed patient. On the other hand, **greed** can also play a role, leading to a desire to "buy the dip" without fully considering the risks. Emotional trading during corrections often results in entering or exiting positions at the wrong time, exacerbating the negative impact of the market correction.

A useful tool for managing emotions during a market correction is to implement **pre-set trading strategies**. This can involve setting predefined entry and exit points, stop-loss orders, and profit-taking strategies. For instance, if an investor believes that a market correction is temporary and that the overall market trend is bullish, they might set a stop-loss order to limit potential losses if the price falls beyond a certain threshold. Having a predetermined exit strategy helps remove emotions from the decision-making process, ensuring that actions are based on logic and analysis, rather than fear or panic. By setting these limits ahead of time, investors can stay on track with their long-term goals and avoid making reactive decisions when the market dips.

Another effective way to stay calm during a market correction is **to maintain a diversified portfolio**. Diversification helps protect investors from the volatility of any single asset, reducing the overall risk of large losses during a market downturn. In the context of cryptocurrency, diversification can mean holding a mix of well-established assets like Bitcoin and Ethereum, along with a selection of altcoins. By spreading risk across multiple assets, investors can avoid putting all their capital into one asset that may be particularly vulnerable during a correction. Additionally, diversification outside of cryptocurrencies, into traditional assets like stocks, bonds, or commodities, can help hedge against the impact of a market correction in the crypto space.

Focusing on the long-term perspective is another critical strategy for staying calm during market corrections. Cryptocurrency markets can be highly volatile, but the long-term trend has historically been upward. Investors who are focused on long-term growth rather than short-term price movements are more likely to weather market corrections successfully. It is essential to remember that corrections are temporary, and if the underlying fundamentals of the asset remain strong, the market is likely to rebound over time. Investors should avoid getting caught up in daily price fluctuations and instead concentrate on their long-term strategy and investment thesis. Holding assets that align with their values and investment goals will make it easier to maintain confidence during temporary downturns.

In addition to focusing on the long-term, **doing thorough research** and staying informed can also help investors stay calm. Market corrections can be triggered by a variety of factors, such as macroeconomic changes, regulatory news, or shifts in market sentiment. Having a deep understanding of the assets in which you're invested allows you to better assess whether the correction is part of a broader trend or a temporary setback. Keeping informed about relevant news, project developments, and market analyses helps provide clarity and prevents reactionary decisions based solely on speculation or fear. Understanding the reasons behind a correction allows investors to make more rational decisions about whether to hold, buy, or sell during the dip.

Finally, **patience and discipline** are essential virtues for surviving market corrections. Corrections can be unsettling, but they are a natural part of the investment journey. Those who have the discipline to stick to their strategy and remain patient during short-term dips are often rewarded in the long term. By avoiding the temptation to act impulsively and by adhering to a well-thought-out plan, investors can stay on track and emerge stronger from market corrections.

In conclusion, staying calm during a market correction requires emotional control, a clear strategy, and a long-term perspective. By understanding the cyclical nature of markets, avoiding emotional reactions, and implementing strategies like diversification and pre-set trading plans, investors can better manage the risks associated with market fluctuations. Maintaining patience and discipline during corrections will help investors avoid making costly mistakes and position themselves for future success in the dynamic cryptocurrency market.

Chapter 8: Risk Management Strategies for the Bull Run

A cryptocurrency bull run presents significant opportunities for investors, but it also comes with increased risk. As prices surge and market enthusiasm grows, the temptation to take on more risk can be overwhelming. However, failing to manage risk during a bull run can lead to substantial losses if the market experiences a sudden correction or downturn. In this chapter, we will explore effective risk management strategies tailored to the unique dynamics of a bull market. By understanding how to balance potential gains with the risks involved, investors can position themselves for success while minimizing the impact of inevitable market fluctuations.

Risk management in a bull market is not just about avoiding losses but also about protecting profits and ensuring that investments align with long-term goals. During a bull run, the market can become highly speculative, with prices driven by hype, emotions, and market sentiment rather than fundamentals. This environment can cause prices to become overinflated, and without proper risk management, investors may find themselves buying into assets at unsustainable levels. Therefore, it is crucial to have a structured plan in place to control risk, define entry and exit points, and utilize tools such as stop-loss orders and portfolio diversification to ensure that potential losses are limited and that gains are secured as prices rise.

In this chapter, we will discuss a range of strategies designed to help investors manage risk effectively during a bull run. These strategies include the use of position sizing, setting stop-loss and take-profit orders, diversifying the portfolio, and applying dollar-cost averaging. Additionally, we will cover the importance of maintaining a disciplined approach and avoiding the common pitfalls of FOMO (fear of missing out) and emotional decision-making that can arise during periods of rapid market growth. By following a systematic approach to risk management, investors can protect their capital and make more informed decisions, ensuring that they are not only participating in the bull run but also navigating it with confidence and resilience.

Diversification: Spreading the Risk

Diversification is one of the most fundamental and effective strategies for managing risk in any investment portfolio, including cryptocurrency. In a highly volatile market like cryptocurrency, where assets can experience extreme price fluctuations within short periods, diversification acts as a safeguard, helping to reduce the potential negative impact of market swings on the overall portfolio. By spreading investments across different assets, sectors, or strategies, investors can mitigate risk and improve the potential for stable, long-term returns. In this article, we will explore the concept of diversification, its importance, and how it can be applied effectively to cryptocurrency portfolios.

At its core, diversification is about not putting all your eggs in one basket. In the context of cryptocurrency, this means investing in a variety of digital assets rather than focusing on a single cryptocurrency. Cryptocurrencies, particularly smaller altcoins, can be highly volatile, with some coins rising rapidly in value while others may experience significant declines. By spreading investments across multiple cryptocurrencies, investors reduce their exposure to the price fluctuations of any one asset. For example, if an investor places all their funds into a single cryptocurrency like Bitcoin or Ethereum and the price of that asset falls, the entire portfolio can suffer. However, if the same investor diversifies their investments into multiple coins, such as Bitcoin, Ethereum, Cardano, Solana, and Polkadot, the risk of large losses is reduced because the performance of these assets is often not directly correlated.

One of the key benefits of diversification is **reducing correlation**. In investment terms, correlation refers to how the price movements of two assets are related. If two assets are highly correlated, meaning their prices move in the same direction, they are exposed to similar market forces, and investing in both does not reduce overall risk. However, if the assets are less correlated or even negatively correlated, their price movements may offset one another. In the case of cryptocurrency, not all coins react the same way to market events. For example, Bitcoin, as the market leader, often drives the general trend of the market, but smaller altcoins can sometimes behave differently. Some may rise in value during a Bitcoin correction, while others may follow Bitcoin's movements. By diversifying into different cryptocurrencies that respond to market factors in different ways, investors can lower the overall volatility of their portfolio.

Another important aspect of diversification in cryptocurrency is **sector diversification**. The crypto market consists of more than just coins used as a store of value or a medium of exchange. It also includes a wide range of blockchain projects focusing on areas such as decentralized finance (DeFi), gaming, supply chain solutions, and privacy. For example, investing in both Bitcoin (a store of value) and Chainlink (a provider of decentralized oracle services) exposes investors to different use cases of blockchain technology. Additionally, other sectors like DeFi platforms (such as Uniswap or

Aave) and non-fungible tokens (NFTs) are rapidly growing sectors with substantial growth potential. By diversifying across various sectors within the cryptocurrency space, investors can tap into multiple areas of growth, making their portfolios more robust and less dependent on the performance of any single sector.

Incorporating **traditional assets** into a cryptocurrency portfolio is another form of diversification that can further spread risk. While cryptocurrencies are an emerging and high-risk asset class, traditional assets like stocks, bonds, and real estate are more established and typically behave differently in market cycles. For instance, when the cryptocurrency market is experiencing a downturn, traditional assets like gold or government bonds may perform better, providing stability and offsetting losses in the crypto market. Additionally, including traditional investments in a crypto portfolio can reduce the overall volatility and increase the chances of earning a consistent return. A diversified portfolio that includes both cryptocurrencies and traditional assets provides a balanced approach to risk management, offering protection during bear markets while still allowing participation in the high-growth potential of the crypto space.

Dollar-cost averaging (DCA) is another strategy that complements diversification in cryptocurrency. DCA involves investing a fixed amount of money at regular intervals, regardless of the asset's price. This approach prevents investors from making decisions based on short-term price fluctuations and reduces the risk of entering the market at a peak. For example, if an investor plans to allocate $1,000 to cryptocurrency each month, they would invest $1,000 in various cryptocurrencies, regardless of the market price. Over time, this approach helps smooth out the impact of market volatility and ensures that the investor is consistently buying into the market, regardless of whether prices are high or low. DCA works well alongside diversification because it allows the investor to slowly build a diversified portfolio over time without making large, risky bets on short-term price movements.

Finally, diversification is not just about selecting different assets—it's also about regularly **rebalancing** the portfolio. As the value of individual cryptocurrencies fluctuates, their relative weight within the portfolio changes. Without periodic rebalancing, a portfolio can become overly concentrated in one asset as its value increases, leading to an increased level of risk. For example, if Bitcoin grows significantly in value, it may make up a larger portion of the portfolio than initially planned, while smaller altcoins may become a smaller portion. Rebalancing the portfolio on a regular basis ensures that the asset allocation aligns with the investor's risk tolerance and long-term objectives, keeping the portfolio balanced and diversified.

In conclusion, diversification is a powerful strategy for managing risk in the cryptocurrency market. By spreading investments across multiple cryptocurrencies, sectors, and even traditional assets, investors can reduce their exposure to individual asset price fluctuations and mitigate overall portfolio risk. Sector diversification and the inclusion of non-correlated assets, such as traditional investments, can enhance portfolio stability. Additionally, using strategies like dollar-cost averaging and regular rebalancing ensures that the portfolio remains balanced and aligned with long-term goals. In a market as volatile as cryptocurrency, diversification is an essential tool for protecting capital while still positioning for growth and potential profits.

Setting Stop-Loss Orders

A stop-loss order is an essential tool in risk management, particularly in volatile markets like cryptocurrency, where prices can swing dramatically in short periods. It is a pre-set instruction to sell a cryptocurrency once its price falls to a certain level, helping investors limit potential losses. While the primary function of a stop-loss order is to protect the investor from large losses, it can also be used to lock in profits and protect gains when prices are rising. Understanding how to set effective stop-loss orders is key to managing risk, maintaining discipline, and preserving capital, especially during periods of high volatility such as bull markets or market corrections.

A **stop-loss order** works by automatically triggering a sale of a cryptocurrency when its price falls to or below a pre-determined threshold. For example, if you purchase a cryptocurrency for $10,000 and set a stop-loss at $9,000, the stop-loss order will automatically execute a sell order if the price drops to $9,000. This type of order removes the need for constant monitoring, as it ensures that losses are capped without needing to react quickly in times of market downturns. By setting a stop-loss order, an investor can protect themselves from further declines in price that might occur during periods of extreme volatility.

There are several types of stop-loss orders that investors can use, depending on their needs and trading strategies. The **basic stop-loss** is a market order that sells the asset at the best available price once the stop price is triggered. This type of order is straightforward but may not always guarantee the exact price at which the asset is sold, especially in fast-moving markets where prices fluctuate rapidly. The **stop-limit order**, on the other hand, sets a stop price and a limit price. When the stop price is triggered, a limit order is placed at the specified limit price or better. While this offers more control over the price at which the asset is sold, it also carries the risk of the order not being filled if the asset's price drops too quickly and fails to reach the limit price.

The **trailing stop-loss** is a more advanced version of the stop-loss order that allows investors to set a stop price relative to the highest market price reached since the order was placed. For example, if an investor sets a trailing stop-loss with a 10% margin, the stop price will adjust upward as the asset's price rises, maintaining a 10% buffer below the highest price. This allows investors to lock in profits as the price increases, while still having protection in place if the price begins to fall. Trailing stop-losses are particularly useful in volatile markets like cryptocurrency, where prices can increase rapidly before experiencing a correction. This order type offers flexibility, as it allows investors to protect profits in bullish markets while still providing downside protection in the event of a market downturn.

When setting a stop-loss order, it's crucial to **determine the appropriate stop price**. This involves assessing the asset's volatility, historical price movement, and overall market conditions. A stop-loss that is too tight can result in being prematurely stopped out due to minor fluctuations in price, while a stop-loss that is too wide may not provide adequate protection against a significant market decline. For instance, if the cryptocurrency is experiencing high volatility, a wider stop-loss may be appropriate to avoid being triggered by normal market fluctuations. Conversely, in a less volatile market, a tighter stop-loss can be used to protect gains more effectively.

Another important consideration is **position sizing**. A stop-loss order works best when combined with effective position sizing. The idea is to ensure that the loss incurred if the stop-loss is triggered is a small percentage of the overall portfolio, not exceeding the investor's risk tolerance. For example, if an investor is willing to risk 2% of their total portfolio on a trade, they should calculate the amount of cryptocurrency to buy based on that risk and set the stop-loss accordingly. Position sizing helps prevent excessive losses in a single trade, making stop-loss orders even more effective at protecting overall portfolio health.

While stop-loss orders are a powerful tool for managing risk, it's important to keep in mind that they are not foolproof. In markets with **extreme volatility**, prices can gap down, meaning they drop past the stop-loss level without executing the order at the desired price. This is more common in assets with lower liquidity or during periods of market panic. To mitigate this risk, investors may choose to use stop-limit orders, though these also come with their own set of challenges, such as the order not being executed if the asset's price falls too quickly.

It's also important for investors to remember that **stop-loss orders should not replace good research and strategy**. While stop-losses provide protection, they should be used in conjunction with a well-thought-out investment plan. Setting stop-loss orders arbitrarily without understanding the market's behavior, asset fundamentals, or the investor's risk tolerance can lead to premature sell-offs or missed opportunities. Stop-loss orders are just one part of a broader risk management strategy that includes proper asset allocation, diversification, and regular portfolio reviews.

In conclusion, stop-loss orders are an essential tool for managing risk in cryptocurrency trading. They offer an automated way to limit losses and protect profits, helping investors navigate volatile markets with greater confidence. By understanding the different types of stop-loss orders—basic, stop-limit, and trailing stop-loss—and determining the appropriate stop price based on the asset's volatility and market conditions, investors can effectively manage their risk. When combined with proper position sizing and a well-defined strategy, stop-loss orders can significantly enhance an investor's ability to navigate the ups and downs of the cryptocurrency market while safeguarding their capital.

Taking Profits at the Right Time

Taking profits at the right time is a crucial part of a successful investment strategy, especially in volatile markets like cryptocurrency. The cryptocurrency market is known for its sharp price movements, both upwards and downwards, making it essential to have a strategy in place for locking in profits while managing risk. However, knowing when to take profits is not always straightforward. Many investors struggle with timing—either holding on for too long and missing out on potential gains, or selling too early and leaving money on the table. In this article, we will explore the key strategies and principles for taking profits at the right time, ensuring that you maximize returns while protecting your investments.

The first step in effectively taking profits is to set clear **profit-taking goals** from the outset. Before entering any trade, it is essential to define your profit target, based on factors such as market analysis, the cryptocurrency's potential, and your investment goals. Setting a predetermined target removes emotion from the equation and ensures that you are making rational decisions. For example, an investor may set a target to sell a portion of their holdings when the asset increases by 20%, or they might choose to take profits in stages as the price increases. This approach ensures that you are consistent in your decision-making, rather than chasing short-term market movements or making impulsive decisions based on FOMO (fear of missing out) or market sentiment.

One effective strategy for taking profits in a volatile market is **scaling out** of a position. This involves selling a portion of your holdings at different price points as the asset appreciates. By selling in increments, you can secure profits while still maintaining exposure to the asset in case the price continues to rise. For instance, you might decide to sell 25% of your holdings once the price has increased by 20%, another 25% at 40%, and so on. This allows you to lock in gains while still benefiting from potential upside. Scaling out also helps to reduce the risk of selling too early, as it ensures that you are capturing profits along the way without committing to selling all at once.

Trailing stop orders are another useful tool for taking profits while maintaining upside potential. A trailing stop order is a type of stop-loss order that adjusts upward as the price of the cryptocurrency rises. It sets a stop price a fixed percentage below the market price, ensuring that if the price falls, your position will be automatically sold to protect your gains. For example, if you buy a cryptocurrency at $100 and set a trailing stop of 10%, the stop price will adjust upward as the price increases. If the price rises to $120, your stop price would move to $108 (10% below $120). If the price then falls to $108, the order is triggered, and you lock in a profit of $8 per coin. This strategy allows you to capture profits as the price rises while still giving the asset room to appreciate without prematurely selling.

Another important concept in taking profits at the right time is **avoiding greed**. Cryptocurrency markets are often fueled by hype and excitement, especially during bull runs, which can lead to greed and overconfidence. When an asset's price rises rapidly, it can be tempting to hold on for even higher gains, hoping that the price will continue to increase indefinitely. However, this mindset can be dangerous, as markets can reverse quickly, leading to missed opportunities or significant losses. It is important to stick to your profit-taking plan and avoid getting caught up in the psychological aspects of trading, such as FOMO or fear of leaving profits on the table. Greed often leads investors to hold onto positions too long, ultimately resulting in a sell-off when the market corrects. By setting clear profit-taking targets and adhering to your plan, you can prevent emotional decisions from jeopardizing your gains.

Market conditions and **technical indicators** can also play a significant role in deciding when to take profits. In a strong bull market, prices may continue to rise for an extended period, allowing for more gradual profit-taking. However, during periods of heightened volatility or market corrections, prices can reverse quickly, making it essential to act swiftly. Technical analysis tools, such as support and resistance levels, moving averages, and RSI (Relative Strength Index), can help you identify optimal points to take profits. For example, if a cryptocurrency is approaching a key resistance level where price has historically struggled to break through, it may be a good time to take profits, as the price could face downward pressure. Similarly, if the RSI indicates that an asset is overbought, this may suggest that it is time to take profits before a potential price correction.

Tax considerations should also be factored into your profit-taking strategy. Cryptocurrency profits are subject to taxation in many jurisdictions, and understanding the tax implications of taking profits is essential for effective financial planning. Depending on your country's tax laws, holding an asset for longer than a year may qualify you for long-term capital gains tax, which is generally lower than short-term capital gains tax. If you anticipate needing to sell assets in the near future, it may be worth considering the tax impact of selling in the short term versus the long term. Consulting with a tax advisor can help you understand how your trades will be taxed and whether it makes sense to delay taking profits for tax efficiency.

Lastly, **staying disciplined** is critical in the process of taking profits. Markets can be unpredictable, and the fear of missing out on additional gains can often cloud judgment. By sticking to your profit-taking strategy, you ensure that you are making decisions based on careful analysis and planning, rather than being swayed by emotional reactions or market noise. Maintaining discipline during both bull and bear markets helps to preserve capital, protect profits, and avoid making costly mistakes driven by emotional impulses.

In conclusion, taking profits at the right time is a key component of a successful investment strategy, particularly in the high-risk, high-reward world of cryptocurrency. By setting clear profit targets, utilizing strategies like scaling out and trailing stops, and avoiding emotional reactions, investors can maximize returns and protect gains. Adhering to a well-thought-out plan, staying disciplined, and considering market conditions and technical indicators will help ensure that profits are locked in at the optimal time, allowing investors to take advantage of the growth potential in the crypto market while mitigating the risks associated with volatility.

Chapter 9
The Role of Decentralized Finance (DeFi)

Decentralized Finance (DeFi) has emerged as one of the most transformative innovations in the cryptocurrency and blockchain space, fundamentally altering the way financial systems operate. Unlike traditional financial systems that rely on intermediaries such as banks, brokers, and payment processors, DeFi leverages blockchain technology to create open, permissionless, and decentralized financial services. These services include lending, borrowing, trading, and investing, all conducted without the need for centralized institutions. In this chapter, we will explore the role of DeFi in the broader cryptocurrency ecosystem, examining how it functions, its benefits, challenges, and how it is reshaping traditional financial systems.

The core idea behind DeFi is to enable individuals to engage in financial activities directly with one another, eliminating the need for centralized authorities. DeFi protocols are built on blockchain platforms, primarily Ethereum, which supports smart contracts—self-executing contracts with predefined terms. These smart contracts enable decentralized applications (DApps) to automate and facilitate financial transactions. The decentralized nature of these platforms ensures that they are accessible to anyone with an internet connection, regardless of geographic location or financial status, democratizing access to financial services. By removing intermediaries, DeFi aims to increase transparency, reduce costs, and make financial services more efficient and inclusive.

Despite its rapid growth, DeFi is still in its early stages and faces several challenges, including security risks, regulatory uncertainty, and scalability concerns. However, its potential to disrupt the traditional finance industry is undeniable. From decentralized exchanges (DEXs) to automated market makers (AMMs) and liquidity pools, DeFi offers a wide range of services that could provide individuals with greater control over their financial assets. In this chapter, we will dive deeper into the various components of DeFi, discuss the risks and rewards associated with it, and analyze its future potential as it continues to evolve and gain traction among users and institutional investors alike.

DeFi: What It Means for the Crypto Ecosystem

Decentralized Finance (DeFi) has become a central pillar of the cryptocurrency ecosystem, providing a new paradigm for financial services that challenges the traditional centralized banking model. Built on blockchain technology, DeFi leverages smart contracts to create a permissionless and decentralized environment for financial transactions, enabling users to access financial products without the need for banks, brokers, or other intermediaries. This radical shift is transforming not only how financial services are provided but also how value is exchanged, stored, and managed in the digital age. In this article, we will explore what DeFi means for the cryptocurrency ecosystem, examining its features, benefits, challenges, and potential impact on the future of finance.

At its core, DeFi aims to replicate traditional financial services — such as lending, borrowing, trading, insurance, and asset management — using blockchain technology. The most significant advantage of DeFi is its decentralization, which eliminates the need for central authorities and intermediaries. This allows users to interact directly with each other in a peer-to-peer network, cutting down on transaction fees, delays, and the reliance on traditional institutions. For example, decentralized exchanges (DEXs) enable users to trade cryptocurrencies directly with each other without the need for a centralized exchange to match buy and sell orders. This also reduces the risk of fraud or hacks, as users retain control over their assets throughout the process.

Smart contracts play a critical role in the success of DeFi platforms. These self-executing contracts automatically enforce the terms of an agreement, without the need for intermediaries. They are deployed on blockchain networks, primarily Ethereum, where their code is publicly visible, ensuring transparency. Smart contracts are used in various DeFi applications, such as lending and borrowing protocols like Aave and Compound, where users can lend their assets to earn interest or borrow assets against collateral. The use of smart contracts eliminates the need for traditional credit checks, making these services more accessible to a global audience, including the unbanked or underbanked populations. This increased financial inclusion is one of the driving forces behind DeFi's growth, as it provides access to financial services that were previously out of reach for many individuals worldwide.

Another key component of DeFi is **liquidity pools**, which enable users to provide liquidity to decentralized exchanges and earn rewards in the form of trading fees or interest. In traditional finance, liquidity is typically provided by central institutions like market makers or banks, but in DeFi, liquidity pools allow anyone to contribute funds and participate in the market. These pools are powered by automated market makers (AMMs) that use algorithms to determine the price of assets within the pool, eliminating the need for order books. AMMs such as Uniswap, SushiSwap, and Balancer have gained popularity in the DeFi space, offering decentralized platforms for token swaps without the need for a centralized authority to match buyers and sellers.

Despite its transformative potential, DeFi is not without its challenges. **Security** is one of the most significant risks associated with DeFi platforms. Because DeFi protocols are open-source and rely on smart contracts, they are vulnerable to bugs or vulnerabilities in the code. Several high-profile hacks and exploits have occurred in the DeFi space, resulting in the loss of millions of dollars. While developers are constantly working to improve the security and auditability of smart contracts, the risk of security breaches remains a concern for investors and users alike. Additionally, DeFi's lack of regulation creates uncertainty around legal and compliance issues, especially as governments and regulatory bodies begin to scrutinize the space more closely. The absence of clear regulations can make it difficult for institutional investors to fully embrace DeFi, as concerns about regulatory risks remain a barrier to widespread adoption.

Scalability is another challenge facing DeFi, particularly on networks like Ethereum, where high levels of traffic can result in slow transaction times and high gas fees. Ethereum, being the most widely used blockchain for DeFi projects, has seen congestion issues that can make transactions expensive and inefficient. While Ethereum 2.0 aims to address these scalability issues through the transition to proof-of-stake and the introduction of sharding, other blockchain platforms such as Solana, Binance Smart Chain, and Avalanche are also positioning themselves as DeFi-friendly alternatives. These networks promise faster transaction speeds and lower fees, which could help

DeFi reach a broader audience and scale beyond Ethereum's limitations.

DeFi also introduces **new risks** to users, such as the potential for "impermanent loss," which occurs when the value of assets in a liquidity pool fluctuates significantly. If a user provides liquidity to a pool with a pair of assets and one asset appreciates significantly more than the other, they could suffer a loss compared to simply holding the assets in a wallet. Additionally, since many DeFi platforms operate in a decentralized manner, there is no recourse for users in case of disputes, bugs, or hacks, which creates a different set of risks compared to traditional financial services.

The potential **impact of DeFi on the broader financial system** is profound. By offering decentralized alternatives to traditional financial products, DeFi has the ability to challenge and disrupt the existing financial infrastructure. For example, it could reduce the reliance on banks for lending and borrowing, enabling individuals to access capital directly from one another. Moreover, DeFi can democratize investment opportunities, allowing anyone with an internet connection to participate in financial markets, earn interest, or invest in decentralized assets. However, the widespread adoption of DeFi could also create regulatory challenges, as governments and financial institutions work to adapt to the rise of decentralized systems that operate outside traditional control.

In conclusion, DeFi represents a revolutionary shift in the way financial services are provided, offering greater accessibility, transparency, and efficiency. It is empowering individuals to take control of their financial assets without intermediaries, fostering a more inclusive financial ecosystem. However, as with any emerging technology, it is important to approach DeFi with caution, considering the associated risks, such as security vulnerabilities, scalability issues, and regulatory uncertainty. As the DeFi space continues to evolve, it will likely play a critical role in the future of finance, driving innovation and challenging traditional systems in ways we are only beginning to understand.

Lending, Borrowing, and Yield Farming

Lending, borrowing, and yield farming are three key concepts within the world of Decentralized Finance (DeFi), and they are transforming the way individuals and institutions interact with financial markets. These concepts leverage blockchain technology and smart contracts to facilitate financial activities without intermediaries such as banks or lending institutions. In the DeFi ecosystem, users have the opportunity to engage in these activities to earn rewards, gain access to liquidity, and optimize the returns on their cryptocurrency holdings. Understanding how lending, borrowing, and yield farming work is essential for navigating the DeFi space and taking advantage of its unique opportunities.

Lending and borrowing are foundational elements of traditional finance, and they have been seamlessly integrated into the DeFi ecosystem. In traditional systems, banks and financial institutions act as intermediaries, offering loans to borrowers and paying interest to lenders. However, in DeFi, the process is decentralized. Instead of relying on a centralized institution, DeFi lending and borrowing platforms use smart contracts to facilitate peer-to-peer transactions between lenders and borrowers. This system eliminates the need for intermediaries, reduces transaction fees, and increases accessibility to financial services for people who may not have access to traditional banking. In DeFi, lenders can provide their cryptocurrency assets to liquidity pools on lending platforms such as Aave, Compound, or

MakerDAO. In return for lending their assets, they earn interest on their deposits. The interest rates offered by DeFi lending platforms can vary based on supply and demand dynamics, with interest rates often being higher than those offered by traditional banks due to the more efficient, decentralized nature of these platforms.

On the other hand, borrowers can access funds without going through the traditional credit evaluation process. Instead, they provide collateral—typically in the form of cryptocurrency—equal to or greater than the value of the loan they wish to take. For example, on platforms like Aave or Compound, borrowers may need to lock up a certain amount of Ethereum or Bitcoin as collateral to borrow USDT or another stablecoin. The collateralization ensures that lenders are protected, as the borrower's assets can be liquidated if they are unable to repay the loan. This collateralized lending model in DeFi eliminates the need for credit checks or third-party evaluations, making these services more accessible to a global audience, including the unbanked or underbanked populations. This increased financial inclusion is one of the driving forces behind DeFi's growth, as it provides access to financial services that were previously out of reach for many individuals worldwide.

Yield farming, also known as liquidity mining, is another popular activity within the DeFi ecosystem that involves using one's cryptocurrency holdings to earn rewards. Yield farming allows investors to provide liquidity to DeFi platforms in exchange for various incentives, such as tokens, fees, or interest. Yield farming is a way to earn passive income on cryptocurrency holdings by participating in the liquidity pools of decentralized exchanges (DEXs), lending platforms, and other DeFi applications. The concept of yield farming works by incentivizing users to provide liquidity to platforms that facilitate transactions. For instance, users can supply liquidity to decentralized exchanges like Uniswap, SushiSwap, or Balancer, which rely on liquidity pools to enable users to trade cryptocurrencies without a centralized order book. In return for providing liquidity, users earn rewards that can come in the form of trading fees, governance tokens, or other incentives. The rewards can vary depending on the platform and the amount of liquidity provided. Typically, the more liquidity a user provides, the higher the potential yield. Yield farming can be highly profitable, but it also comes with significant risk. The returns are often measured as an annual percentage yield (APY), but the rates can be volatile due to changes in market conditions, liquidity demand, and the assets involved. Yield farming often involves multiple steps, such as staking tokens in a liquidity pool, participating in governance, or reinvesting earnings. In addition to earning rewards, some yield farming strategies also enable users to take part in the governance of DeFi projects by holding governance tokens, which provide voting rights on key decisions about the platform's future.

However, there are risks associated with yield farming, including impermanent loss, which occurs when the value of the assets in the liquidity pool changes relative to each other. For example, if the price of one asset in the pool rises significantly while the price of the other asset falls, liquidity providers may experience a loss compared to simply holding the assets in a wallet. Additionally, since many DeFi platforms operate in a decentralized manner, there is no recourse for users in case of disputes, bugs, or hacks, which creates a different set of risks compared to traditional financial services. The rise of protocols like Compound and Aave has made it easier for users to lend and borrow cryptocurrencies, while projects like Yearn.finance and Harvest Finance have simplified the process of yield farming. These platforms aggregate different yield farming opportunities, optimizing returns for users by automatically moving assets between different liquidity pools to achieve the best yields.

In conclusion, lending, borrowing, and yield farming have become crucial components of the DeFi ecosystem, offering users new ways to generate passive income, access liquidity, and participate in decentralized financial markets. While these activities provide opportunities for significant returns, they also come with risks, including exposure to volatility, impermanent loss, and security vulnerabilities. By understanding how these mechanisms work and the risks involved, users can make informed decisions about how to interact with DeFi platforms, potentially unlocking new financial opportunities in the cryptocurrency space.

How DeFi Can Accelerate the Bull Run

Decentralized Finance (DeFi) has been a game-changer for the cryptocurrency ecosystem, and its rapid growth is expected to play a significant role in accelerating the next bull run. By eliminating traditional intermediaries and providing open, permissionless access to financial services, DeFi has introduced new opportunities for investors, traders, and developers to participate in the market. With its innovative platforms, tools, and incentives, DeFi enhances liquidity, attracts new capital, and fosters an environment ripe for innovation, all of which can contribute to the acceleration of a bull market in the crypto space.

One of the most impactful ways that DeFi can accelerate a bull run is by **increasing liquidity** in the market. Liquidity is a key factor in enabling smooth transactions and price stability, which in turn fuels market growth. DeFi protocols, such as decentralized exchanges (DEXs) and lending platforms, allow users to directly trade, lend, and borrow assets without relying on centralized exchanges or financial institutions. By providing liquidity to these platforms through mechanisms like liquidity pools and automated market makers (AMMs), DeFi participants help facilitate trading and other financial activities, driving up market activity. The increased liquidity ensures that prices can adjust more efficiently to demand, enabling greater price discovery and fueling further bullish momentum.

Another way DeFi accelerates a bull run is through **wider market access**. Traditional financial systems are often limited by geographical and institutional barriers, which can restrict the flow of capital into the market. DeFi eliminates these barriers, providing users worldwide with the ability to access a wide range of financial services, from lending and borrowing to yield farming and staking. As more people from diverse backgrounds are able to participate in DeFi, the market experiences an influx of capital, which drives the demand for cryptocurrencies. The removal of traditional gatekeepers democratizes access to financial products, making it easier for retail investors to engage with the market, thereby increasing the volume of trades and potentially accelerating a bull run.

The incentive structures in DeFi also contribute to market growth. Platforms often reward users for participating in various activities, such as providing liquidity or staking tokens. These rewards are typically in the form of governance tokens, which offer holders a say in the platform's future decisions. The promise of attractive returns, whether from interest rates on lending or yield farming rewards, incentivizes capital inflow into DeFi protocols. This surge in activity can lead to increased demand for underlying assets, further pushing up their prices during a bull run. Furthermore, the compounding rewards that yield farmers earn can result in a **snowball effect**, where the reinvestment of profits into the ecosystem leads to even more liquidity and higher asset prices.

DeFi protocols are also designed to be **interoperable**, meaning that they can communicate and work together across different blockchain networks. This interconnectedness broadens the reach and efficiency of DeFi applications, making it easier for users to move assets between platforms and access a wider range of financial products. With greater interoperability, the DeFi ecosystem becomes more robust, attracting more users and further increasing demand for cryptocurrencies. This broader participation can amplify the effects of a bull run, as the interconnectedness of DeFi platforms helps the entire ecosystem grow at an accelerated pace.

Moreover, the rise of **yield farming** and **liquidity mining** in DeFi creates new opportunities for investors to earn passive income on their holdings, incentivizing more people to hold and participate in the market. As more people engage in yield farming, liquidity increases, helping to stabilize the market and support bullish trends. By providing opportunities for users to earn rewards through these mechanisms, DeFi platforms attract more capital, driving further price appreciation of cryptocurrencies.

Lastly, DeFi platforms encourage **innovation** by enabling new financial products and services. The ability to create customized financial instruments, such as synthetic assets, prediction markets, and decentralized insurance, can attract new participants and use cases, expanding the scope of what's possible in the crypto space. The innovation-driven nature of DeFi platforms fosters a positive feedback loop, where the creation of new products attracts more users, which in turn attracts more liquidity, creating a virtuous cycle that accelerates the bull run.

In conclusion, DeFi plays a crucial role in accelerating the cryptocurrency market's bull run by increasing liquidity, providing global access to financial services, offering attractive incentives, enhancing interoperability, and fostering innovation. As DeFi continues to grow, its influence on the crypto ecosystem will likely become more pronounced, driving increased capital inflows, market participation, and asset prices. By decentralizing finance and creating an open, transparent, and efficient market, DeFi contributes to the overall expansion and maturity of the cryptocurrency space, creating a robust foundation for a sustainable bull run.

Conclusion

As we conclude our exploration of the cryptocurrency landscape and its potential to catalyze the next bull run, it becomes clear that the convergence of technological innovation, decentralized finance, and market dynamics presents a unique opportunity for investors, traders, and developers alike. The emergence of decentralized finance (DeFi) has reshaped the crypto ecosystem, offering more inclusive, transparent, and efficient financial services. In this new decentralized world, the traditional financial system is no longer the sole gatekeeper to wealth creation, and blockchain technology has unlocked endless possibilities for redefining value exchange, governance, and innovation.

Throughout this book, we have discussed key elements of the crypto market and their contributions to the ongoing bull run, from the importance of market cycles and indicators to the role of institutional investors, DeFi protocols, and the critical strategies for maximizing profit while minimizing risk. Understanding these fundamentals equips both seasoned and novice investors with the knowledge to make informed decisions in a rapidly evolving environment. The nature of cryptocurrency markets is inherently volatile, and it's essential to approach these markets with caution, strategy, and an eye toward long-term success.

The crypto ecosystem is maturing, and with it, the tools available to market participants are becoming more sophisticated. As DeFi continues to grow, more people around the world can access financial services that were previously out of reach, bridging gaps in global financial inclusion. At the same time, technological advancements such as the rise of layer 2 scaling solutions, the ongoing Ethereum 2.0 upgrade, and interoperability between blockchains are helping to address some of the challenges the crypto space has faced, including scalability and transaction costs. As these hurdles are overcome, the potential for more widespread adoption becomes even more apparent, and the market's trajectory can continue to accelerate in ways that were once thought impossible.

However, as we move forward into this exciting phase of cryptocurrency's evolution, it is essential to remember that the market is not without its risks. The volatility that defines crypto markets can lead to substantial gains, but also significant losses. Therefore, risk management strategies such as diversification, the use of stop-loss orders, and taking profits at the right time are critical to navigating this landscape effectively. Furthermore, while the decentralized nature of the crypto ecosystem is a fundamental strength, it also presents regulatory and security challenges that will need to be addressed in the coming years. The regulatory environment is still evolving, and staying informed about potential legal developments is important for ensuring that investments remain compliant and secure.

The opportunities presented by cryptocurrency and DeFi are immense, but success requires a disciplined, informed approach. As the market matures, we can expect new technologies, platforms, and financial products to emerge, pushing the boundaries of what is possible and offering exciting prospects for investors. Whether you're looking to participate in the next bull run, explore new DeFi innovations, or secure your financial future through strategic investment, the principles outlined in this book can serve as a foundation for navigating the ever-changing world of cryptocurrency.

In closing, the future of cryptocurrency and decentralized finance is bright, but the journey requires patience, persistence, and a long-term perspective. With the right knowledge, strategy, and mindset, you can take full advantage of the opportunities presented by this dynamic market, whether you're looking to maximize returns, protect your assets, or simply participate in the evolution of the global financial system. The bull run may be just the beginning, and with the rapid advancements in blockchain and DeFi, the possibilities for the future of finance are limitless. As you continue to explore and engage with this exciting space, remember that success in cryptocurrency is not only about timing the market but about embracing innovation, staying disciplined, and adapting to the evolving landscape with confidence.

www.ingramcontent.com/pod-product-compliance
Lightning Source LLC
LaVergne TN
LVHW061526070526
838199LV00009B/393